VOICES of my FATHER
A CONVERSION PROJECT

ANTHONY CARTER

Milligan Books · California

Copyright © 2004 by Anthony Carter
Los Angeles, California
All rights reserved
Printed and bound in the United States of America

Distributed by:
Milligan Books
1425 W. Manchester Blvd., Suite C, Los Angeles, California 90047
(323) 750-3592
(323) 750-2886 Fax

Cover Lay-out and Design by: A3Arts.com Gary Scott
Photography by: Rare Essence Photography Terri Bell

First Printing, April 2004
10 9 8 7 6 5 4 3 2 1

ISBN # 0-9753504-1-2

No part of this book may be reproduced in whole or in part, in any form or by any means, electronic or mechanical, including photocopying, recording or by any information storage and retrieval system, without permission in writing from the author. Direct all inquiries to Milligan Books:

Milligan Books, Inc.
1425 W. Manchester Ave., Suite C, Los Angeles, California 90047
www.milliganbooks.com
(323) 750-3592

Anthony Carter
P. O. Box 56152, Los Angeles, CA 90056
anthonycarter@comcast.net

Book Formatting by Chris Ebuehi/Graphic Options Los Angeles, CA

TABLE OF CONTENTS

ABOUT THE AUTHOR	V	
ACKNOWLEDGMENTS	VII	
CHAPTER ONE	*THE SIGNIFICANT YEARS* 1	
CHAPTER TWO	*DADDY'S WISH* 21	
CHAPTER THREE	*ALARM IN MY HEAD* 29	
CHAPTER FOUR	*REMEMBERING RHONDA* 41	
CHAPTER FIVE	*GOING HOME* 53	
CHAPTER SIX	*SUNSTREET, IGANASIO AND*	
	SUCCESS 65	
CHAPTER SEVEN	*COMPOSURE FOR THE 10TH* 79	
CHAPTER EIGHT	*EMBANKMENT* 93	
CHAPTER NINE	*THE BOX AND DEE DEE FELI* 109	
CHAPTER TEN	*CORRUPTION AND CONFUSION* . . .131	
CHAPTER ELEVEN	*TRANSFORMING* 153	
CHAPTER TWELVE	*POINT BLANK* 179	
CHAPTER THIRTEEN	*DEPARTURE* 203	
CHAPTER FOURTEEN	*SITUATION SUPER BOWL* 219	
CHAPTER FIFTEEN	*DESTINY* .237	
CHAPTER SIXTEEN	*NO CHOICE IN THE MATTER* 249	

About The Author

Anthony Carter is a native of Richmond, Virginia. He is also a graduate of California State University, Los Angeles with a Bachelor of Science degree in Business Administration, Administrative Management with a minor in Economics. He earned a Masters of Arts degree in Ministry, Missiology from Bethany Theological Seminary located in Dothan, Alabama where he graduated Summa Cum Laude. He is also an ABA certified paralegal.

Besides being a writer, Anthony Carter is an urban entrepreneur and the founder, president and CEO of The Conversion Project, Inc., a faith-based nonprofit organization that serves primarily inner city disadvantage males within the Los Angeles area. Mr. Carter is single and resides in Los Angeles, California.

Acknowledgments

First, I must acknowledge God for all reasons, however for the purpose of this book for affording me, even from before inception, the wisdom and discernment that has guided me through, not only the writing of this book, but also this journey called life.

Secondly, I must acknowledge my parents, the late Frank Irvin Carter, Sr. and Helen Christopher Carter Crockett whom instilled in me as a child the basic fabric for manhood and for making me get up early every morning, but also to my mother for sticking by me even though at times my "butt" was not smelling too good.

Third, I must acknowledge my siblings Frank, Jr., Cynthia and Sandra, all of whom had to put up with a lot of me and yet still managed to teach me life altering lessons. I never cease thanking God that He afforded me the opportunity to be your little brother.

Fourth, I must acknowledge Sister Dr. Carma Chinyere Love, whom has continued to remind me over the years that although at times I was in some pretty dark places the Light continued to shine on me.

Finally, I would be remiss if I did not acknowledge all of my friends and family around the world. However, because there are too many of you to name and since I do not want to leave anyone out I won't—but you know who you are. Thank you because each of you have touched my life in profound ways.

Anthony Carter

CHAPTER ONE

THE SIGNIFICANT YEARS

The other day I received a significant letter that contained some rather sound advice. Over the years I have always valued sound advice and can attest I have gotten a lot of it—from various sources. We should always thank God for providing us with people that can give us good counsel, especially those people who know where you are coming from and seem to know where you are going.

God has always led me in my understanding and I thank Him for not only affording me the opportunity to receive desirable advice, but also, for giving me the ability to discern the good instruction from the bad. The letter was from my tenacious mother, who has not written me much over the years, however, history has taught me that advice coming from her has always proved beneficial. As with all mothers, they seem to know us in most ways better than we know ourselves. One might assume that a letter coming from your mother cannot be much different than any other, but this letter symbolized the epitome of wisdom.

That day I was feeling somewhat depressed, lonely, not loved, not cared about, and even neglected by the very people I thought loved me. Suddenly I received an affirmation through my mother's timely advice. Or, was this a revelation? Whatever it was I am sure it was definitely a Divine interposition—instructing me to do something about my condition. I believe this was part of God's predetermined destiny for me. Nevertheless, since I should have done this long ago and did not, I now have the time, inspiration, motivation, not to mention the anointing of God, and I no longer have a choice in the matter.

I am going to tell you about a journey—not always good—not always bad, nonetheless a true story, a testimony you might say. I was born on November 12, 1961 at the Medical College of Virginia in Richmond. I am the youngest of four children, the second son born to the late Frank Irvin Carter, Sr., a laborer, and Helen Christopher Carter, also a laborer turned administrator. My parents were passionate about making a better life for us. They always put the well-being of the family first and we were always provided for.

As far back as I can remember we lived in Jackson Ward, an infamous housing project in Richmond, then considered to be a rough neighborhood. Some called it a ghetto—some called it a slum but all I knew was it was home, and a successful man was pushing dope, pimping or both. Dad worked a lot and was gone most of the time. Unlike then, now I know why—he was trying to work his family out of that economically deprived environment.

Mom, much like in many other African-American households then and today, was the authoritative figure in the house—at least until dad came home. Cynthia (my sister, a year older than me) and I were constantly under my mother's care in those days. We could not go outside much at all, I assume it was for our protection considering all the evil spirits that were so prevalent in that neighborhood. Sandra (my oldest sister) and Junie (my older brother) were already in school. I do not remember them being around the house much at all.

However, I do remember Cynthia being around the house, especially one wretched occasion that will undoubtedly remain in my mind, I am sure, until I separate from this flesh. Mom was hanging clothes on the downstairs line and Cynthia and I were playing upstairs in the kitchen. We had one of those old washing machines with wringers on them. Not unlike any other five and four year old children we too were filled with curiosity.

Yet, unlike me Cynthia was a very intelligent youngster. The more I reminiscence about those days the more I have come to the conclusion that she may have been a little envious of the fact that I was the baby of the family. She put her fingers on the revolving rollers between the wringers of that old washing machine and dared me to do the same. Throughout history many siblings have challenged each other in that manner. Naturally I accepted her challenge with pleasure, only to have my entire arm engulfed by the rollers. The violent forces of that washing machine separated my index finger and thumb from the rest of my hand, also crushing my arm. Then Cynthia just stood there with this stoic expression on her face not doing anything, especially since she was too little to do anything. My mother responded to my agonizing screams, augmented by the excruciating pain that had taken dominion over me, and ran up the stairs, saving my life. I was rushed to the hospital where my little fingers were stitched back to my hand and there I remained for it seemed an eternity with my arm attached to a sling in the air.

In 1965 we moved to Central Gardens, back then you could classify that neighborhood as being middle class for African-Americans. My daddy still was only present late at night and usually was tired when he came home so he spent very little time with us. My parents were both middle children in large families. There were nine children on my father's side of the family and twelve children on my mother's side. They were both raised in Prince Edward County in rural Virginia. My grandparents, on both sides of the family, were virtuous, austere people who raised their children the way my parents raised us with good old-fashioned morals, which is very common with most Southern Baptist families. Proverbs 22:6 tells us to "Train a child in the way he should go, and when he is old he will not depart from it." My parents used stringency in bringing up their children. We knew if they told us to do something, we had better do it, especially if we knew what was good for us. There was no talking back and their instructions to us were non-negotiable. When my father came home, no matter how tired he was, if we had misbehaved at school, or at home, we would get a "whipping" from him, this after we probably had already received one from mom. I did not know it then, but this was the only manner in which my parents knew how to discipline us.

We had to go to Sunday school and church every week. We

had to go to school everyday and bring home good grades. When we got home we had to do our homework and after that there were chores around the house that each of us were assigned. At the end of the week we were given an allowance for our good deeds. I remember my first job—I was about five years old and my father had a huge paper route in Churchill, which was considered then, and still is, one of the roughest neighborhoods in Richmond. The entire family had to wake up before school at around 4:00 A.M. every morning. My job was to fold the newspapers in the car while my brother and older sisters did the actual delivering. Eventually I grew into the position of a deliverer. Although I hated the chore, we did seem to always have more materially than the other kids in the neighborhood.

My father became so skilled in the paper delivering business that he would hire some of the neighborhood youngsters and pay them $100 a week. In the 1960s and 70s that was a lot of money for a kid. At any rate, that paper route has proven to be beneficial in our lives by teaching us responsibility at an early age, and to this very day I still get up about 5:00 A.M. every morning.

My siblings and I also were unaware then that our parents were saving money to better our social and economic status. Mom and dad also had daytime jobs during the early years, both working for a head-wear company. I would go to Cedar Street Memorial Baptist Church Day-Care Center until mom or dad came home.

One afternoon in 1968 before I started the first grade, I remember watching the tears stream down my mother's face, apparently caused by the grievous images on television. My mother and I were watching the funeral of the Reverend Dr. Martin Luther King, Jr. The significant contributions this man made to society at that time were then beyond my comprehension. Yet in time I came to understand who this complex man was and what he and his vigorous non-violent message represented.

In the fall of that year I started the first grade at Central Gardens Elementary School. Ms. Michaels was my first grade teacher. This monumental event was much anticipated. I had been waiting forever for that day to come and it was more than I had imagined. Junie (my brother) was delegated to make sure that I made it to and from school safely; however, there was a problem that surfaced right away. It seemed that since I never got an opportunity to act up at home, school represented a safe haven for me to do so. This rebellious, misbehaving pattern would stick with me throughout my entire school days.

The school seemed enormous then and the classes seemed even larger. All of my friends were in my class then, "Bay Bay," Stoddie, Michael, Wayne, Malcolm, "Gay Gay," Kim, Arlette, "Grump", and Dana. I remember the first time I got into trouble. Dana and I were walking on the tables after Ms. Michaels had gone out of the classroom. Both of us had to go to the office to see the Principal, Ms. Jones, who all the kids thought was the most evil person in the world.

She had established a renowned reputation for herself as a stern disciplinarian. We waited outside her office until we were called in one by one. I was instructed to pull my pant leg up where I was lashed ten times with a leather strap. This was a punishment that every kid in Central Gardens knew about and feared. Each of us was given a note that was intended to inform our parents of what we had done and what punishment we had received.

The letter was undoubtedly the worst punishment I could ever have received because I knew what my parents were going to do to me when they got home. Dad was always tired by the time he got home, plus he had probably stopped by Ms. Blanches', which was also known as the "shot house," for a couple of drinks, so it was extremely difficult to predict what his reaction was going to be. My mother had this intuitive ability to make him react in a desired fashion. She, as usual, told my inebriated father that I had gotten into trouble at school. My father came to my room and told me to take off all of my clothes. He said that he would be back after he had gotten a switch off of the tree. Fortunately that night, like many others, he was too intoxicated and exhausted and never made it back.

In terms of him disciplining us there were many nights like that one. In fact there were many nights when dad would come home and just pass out. He would not say anything about our bad behavior usually until he had gotten drunk. Eventually he would get around to giving us our "whipping." However in looking back at all those whippings we received, I would not recommend this as the only way to chasten a child. I know this pummel method did not suffice in my case and, in my opinion, there are other more effective chastising methods to teach and nurture children.

Sometimes I wonder whether those whippings were my parents' means of releasing stress. On numerous occasions I had personally observed my parents vent their frustrations through mild violence—if there exists such an emotion. God only knows my siblings and I received a lot of whippings. But my siblings never really got into trouble that much. So I am not sure why I did, although I do know that I received most of the disciplining during those days. One might suspect that since I received the bulk of the disciplining that my parents issued, I would have turned out better than my siblings. Yet that did not happen either.

In the early 1970's just before I was about to start the fourth grade there was much talk amongst the older people about something called "Busing," or "Desegregation." It was unclear to us what these terms meant, however, we were aware that it was to affect our lives. Unlike my brother and two older sisters, I would not be attending Central Gardens Elementary for the fourth and the fifth grades. I had to attend Highlands Springs Elementary School about fifteen miles from the neighborhood. The kids that lived on the other side of the street went to another school. The Henrico County School Board turned Central Gardens Elementary into only a sixth grade school so I knew that one day I would return to the only school that I had ever known. Besides my parents had taught us that no matter what unexpected turns our lives took, we could, and would adapt and go forward.

During this period of uncertainty many of the kids in the neighborhood were separated. However sometimes change gives reason for optimism, especially since many of us had never been out of the neighborhood. Nonetheless this would be my opportunity to ride the "Big Cheese," also known as a school bus. The first day we got off of the bus at Highland Springs Elementary we noticed something that we had never seen before, all these little white kids running around. We did not know what to expect, until then our entire world had been our own ethnicity.

Central Gardens was a neighborhood made up of only African-Americans and that school's population consisted entirely of the African-Americans that lived in our community. There were African-American teachers, administrators, faculty members and culture. Now to be propelled against our will into a school made up of predominately whites and white culture was frightening. I now believe we were experiencing a fear of the unknown.

However I quickly adjusted, thanks to my fourth grade instructor Ms. Chenier who was extremely helpful during this transformation. The school was much nicer, cleaner and bigger than Central Gardens. The food was better and the library was bigger and had more books. My friends and I got to participate in a variety of sports that had eluded us at Central Gardens. We met a lot of interesting people there. Most of us developed relationships that have lasted until this very day. At Highland Springs Elementary I discovered many unknowns about myself, a distinctive chastity—a virtue that my previous three teachers had told me about. However I just thought they were doing their jobs. I soon discovered that there was definitely a Divine calling and a predetermined destiny for my life.

Almost immediately I was put into a higher grade to study English and Mathematics. Ms. Chenier was the first teacher who really exploited the fact that I possessed exceptional talent in those subjects. As I ponder that situation I believe those teachers were affording me an opportunity to advance one complete grade. However I wanted to remain with my peers. The idea of leaving them was petrifying. My parents did not make me do it so I rejected their proposition.

As I write about that lost opportunity I cannot help but wonder how my life may have been different had I focused on the academics at that tender age? I wish that I could speak with Ms. Chenier just to hear what it was that she saw in me at that point in my life. I can honestly attest that my memories of her are fond. There were other teachers and later in college, instructors who were, as they should have been, very intricate in the developmental stages of my secular knowledge.

Two years later I was back at Central Gardens School, this time for the sixth grade. That period of my life began to mold me into the person that I was, until I found my true identity. I have some very vivid memories of the sixth grade, partly because that was the beginning of my formative years and partly because there in the sixth grade was where I met my first puppy love.

Although I was only twelve years old, Central Gardens School at that point in my life was the center of the universe. In that grade the girls began to notice the boys and they would let us know it. I was an extremely popular personality amongst my peers, mostly because I was still getting into a lot of trouble. However by then the trouble had escalated into skipping school, being disrespectful to basically every authority figure, taking drugs, smoking cigarettes, girl chasing, and lots of drinking.

There was this new girl that everyone was talking about. They called her "Arnie," and although I had never seen or met her I felt that I knew her. I remember my friends telling me about her smile, her personality, her complexion, her eyes and just how nice she was. Nobody had anything bad to say about her, which in itself was a rarity.

All this talk of Arnie made me curious. I had become infatuated by their descriptions of her and I wanted desperately to meet her. Straightforward as I was, I asked my beloved cousin Gail who was in the band with Arnie to introduce us. She did and my world has never been the same since. She was the girl of my dreams and I believed that she felt the same about me. We were inseparable for a long time. She mentioned to me once that she had been just as interested in meeting me as I was in meeting her. She was a spiritually beautiful girl, as attractive a girl as I had ever met. This was genuine puppy love and the first real love that I had ever known. Secrets about my sensuality were revealed that I was previously unaware existed. We talked about everything from our families to how we intended to spend the remaining days of our lives together.

Along with Arnie came a regiment amount of trouble. Our parents felt that we were too young and were spending too much of our time together. There were occasions when my family would go to the shopping mall near where she lived and I would sneak away to her house, sometimes staying over there until my family had to come and look for me. I loved my Arnie and often marvel how my life may have been had we continued our fairy-tale puppy love affair. She was such a complement to everything about me. Everyone said we looked well together and to this very day people still associate us together. There was a lot of cultivation that took place in our lives during that time. Our relation bred a standard of love and trust that has reverberated ever since. I truly believe that no matter what the circumstances in our lives, there was definitely a Divine intent for our paths to intertwine.

Life was speeding up on the home front. Sandra had started dating Comer Best, a star defensive end for the Highland Springs High School football team. I remember one night he brought her home late and my father pulled out a .38 caliber revolver from his rather large gun collection and stuck it to Comer's head. He told him if he ever brought his daughter home late again he would blow his brains out. I veritably believe that he meant it. That was not the first time that I saw my father brandish a firearm. As a matter of fact he had a fascination for them and owned quite a few. He even brought my brother and me rifles and taught us how to use them at an early age. We would go hunting whenever we went to the country where my grandparents lived.

VOICES OF MY FATHER

They were really exceptional people and to this very day, I can honestly say that all of my grandparents had a profound effect on my life. We addressed my father's parents as Big Ma and Big Pa. We knew my mother's parents as Grandma and Grandpa. They were all classic old country folk whom lived mostly off of the land. All were tobacco farmers and raised pigs, chickens, cows, horses and mules. I hated going to the country because they made us work hard whenever we went there. Junie would get dropped off up there when school was out in the summertime and stay there until school began in the fall.

When we would have family dinners my Big Ma would go out into the front yard and grab a live chicken and wring its neck. Afterwards, the headless chicken, still alive, would run around the yard for a while although it seemed more like an eternity. After the chicken finally dropped dead, Big Ma would dress the chicken, put it in boiling water, pluck it, cook it and it would be on the dinner table. Those were some of the most delicious-tasting chickens I have ever eaten. And seeing how those chickens made their way to the dinner table sure gave me a better understanding of the ecosystem.

Big Ma was a beautiful virtuous woman with golden skin, long black silky hair, and a strong personality. She lived the longest of any of my grandparents and I loved her dearly. Big Pa was a very keen man and I was under the impression that he knew everything and in trying to understand him, I came to understand my father better. Big Pa was the inheritor of some two hundred acres. He knew where every tree was located and used every inch of that farmland. The old man worked from sun-up to sundown and managed to out-live three of his four sons. He would harvest tobacco in the summertime and kill hogs in the winter for those were his primary sources of income. I remember all those years going to the country just to watch because I was too young to participate. My aunts, uncles, cousins, and of course my parents and siblings, farmed it seemed every crop I can think of.

Big Pa had a special relationship with all of his grandchildren, especially my brother Junie although he would notice little things about each of us that even our parents would not—then he would playfully expose them. He had a great sense of humor and he was an extremely spiritual man, serving as deacon at High Rock Baptist Church.

My uncle John was my father's older brother. He had never left home, when my Big Ma died he was still there. In the early 1940's my uncle John was diagnosed at an early age as having a mental disability. In fact my father's brother Henry had died in an insane asylum at the age of forty-four. Apparently he had been committed there when he was just fourteen years old. Uncle John and my father shared a uniquely special bond. I would often hear them talking about their other brother Sam who in the 1950's had also died at the age of forty-four. He had been the victim of a racially motivated beating by the hands of the Klu Klux Klan, who then placed him on a railroad track and left him for dead. They would talk about how my grandparents were really doing and how my aunts, who all lived in New Jersey, were treating them. Uncle John was also Big Pa's scapegoat. Whenever something went wrong around that farm it was uncle John who took the blame.

Often I wondered why he never left home. However that life was all he ever knew and quite frankly all he ever wanted to know. His entire life was dedicated to serving his parents. He never married and I do not think that he ever really wanted to. When uncle John would come to Richmond for a weekend or a holiday my father would try to set him up with a date. However I do not believe that any of my father's efforts proved fruitful. As I ponder uncle John's desolate life and his diligent service to his parents, it is evident that God has something very special for him in Heaven.

Throughout all those years of going back and forth to the country, there were many instances that will forever take residence in my mind. However nothing will ever have such a lasting impression as the way those people loved God. They studied the Bible and fellowshipped with their neighbors unlike anything I have ever witnessed before or since. The Disciple John wrote in 1 John 1:7, "But if we walk in the light, as He is in the light, we have fellowship with one another, and the blood of Jesus, his Son, purifies us from all sin." I remember going to yearly revivals at High Rock Baptist Church every fourth Sunday in August. There, my entire family would come together once a year and praise God in the most profound way. Each night of the week there was another fire and brimstone preacher in the pulpit. I was not always certain what their messages were, but even as a young child I could sense the presence of the Holy Spirit. After those services there would be a tremendous amount of fellowshipping and eating with the congregation. There was so much food that hundreds of people could eat all afternoon and have leftovers all week.

The fourth Sunday in August was also the occasion that we had an opportunity to see my cousins from around the United States. All the kids would compare how much we'd grown over the year. I have some very personable and beautiful cousins and to this very day most of us have remained very close. My cousin Michael was a very entangled part of my childhood. We were the same age and extremely close. Although Michael and I have grown apart over our adult years I think of him often, and I know that one day we will have an opportunity to put our busy schedules aside and reminisce about our different journeys.

The kids would catch the first ride back to the farm from the revivals and we would play games such as hide and seek and catching lightning bugs. We would gather together and sing "Jackson Five" tunes and laugh all night. Big Ma and Big Pa usually were the last two to come in from church, which was our signal to shut up and go to bed.

My father would be sitting and drinking in a car with his favorite cousin Jimmy and they would show up sometime in the afternoon, usually drunk, only to be chastened by my father's five older sisters. My mother would not say too much because she knew how mad that would make him. Like most men he was insecure about his shortcomings. When my father was drunk he liked to drive the car. There were numerous occasions when he would get behind the wheel and attempt to drive with the entire petrified family in the car. We knew he was too drunk to drive but the more we told him the more he wanted to prove that he was not. However we always made it home safely—which can only be attributed to the grace of God. I believe in demons and evil spirits and I know they took dominion over my father during his drunkenness. The fourth Sunday in August also marked the day my brother would come back to Richmond. We would say our yearly farewells to all of my aunts, uncles and cousins, who would go back to East Orange. At least for the year we would go our separate ways.

VOICES OF MY FATHER

My grandparents, unlike my Big Parents, seemed to always be at odds. My mother had six brothers and four of them lived within walking distance from where they grew up. All were extremely skilled farmers. As did my father's parents, my grandparents owned lots of land and until this very day my uncles and cousins are still farming. Grandpa was a dignified man who also was blessed with a great sense of humor. He was always in control of that massive farm. Whenever a major decision was in order regarding the operation of it, my uncles would always consult him because his farm was twice the size of Big Pa's and he had more equipment and livestock. There were always a lot of people around and new faces each time we went there. I was precariously unsure of what was going on around there; however, it was organized and they were solemn about what they were doing. My grandfather was at the center of all of it. He died in that same chair on the front porch that he liked to sit in for hours and wave at all the cars that went by.

My cousins Gerald and Dennis, who were closest to me in age, used to take me to all the remote areas of that farm. They would ask me about the city life, and I was just as intrigued and fascinated by their country living. They had unlimited access to everything on that immense farm. They took me to remote areas that I never imagined existed on this earth, let alone on a farm. They would show me ways to survive on the environment, things far beyond the comprehension of a city boy and even though we all were the same age, they were bigger, stronger and faster than me. They were hard workers and possessed a vigilant approach to life that most people take for granted.

Grandma, in my biased opinion, was the best cook I have ever known. I mean she could really cook well. She was also gifted in the area of quilting and made many of them. She too had a close and personal relationship with all of her grandchildren. This was a tremendous feat considering there were a lot of us. Every year she gave each of us the same gift. At Christmas I was going to receive a package of Fruit of the Loom underwear. My siblings and I would joke about what Grandma was going to give us at Christmas.

During the 1960s and 70's in the summertime I loved going to Grandma's house. She was a master at making homemade ice cream. Grandma knew everything about every soap opera on television. She would talk to herself about them often. I have vivid memories of my grandfather telling her "shut up, woman." Grandpa died when I was around nine years old and his funeral was more like a family reunion. There must have been two hundred people there with cars lined up for miles. Never in my life had I been in the presence of so many people.

In the mid 1970's back in the neighborhood, once you were old enough to graduate into Fairfield Junior High School, you were considered to be a big boy. When I think of Fairfield, I cannot help but think of Ms. Lane, who was my seventh grade homeroom and biology teacher. She was a lovely Anglo woman in her mid-twenties. Just like most of my previous teachers, she seemed to take a genuine interest in my learning. She helped considerably, especially with the sciences, which I hated with a passion. Ms. Lane was considered by most to be relatively strict and many of my friends did not like her. However I did like her immensely and I was fortunate to never experience her negative side. I have always since evaluated my instructors against the standard that she undoubtedly set. There are vivid memories of her friendship with Mr. Firebaugh, who became my eighth grade homeroom teacher.

Mr. Firebaugh was my most tantalizing instructor during

those developmental years. I am sure he thought I was perplexing however he told me once that I was the most intelligent student he had ever encountered. However I saw him as one of my first true role models. He was always dressed to impress, and his speech was very articulate. He had this intuitive big brotherly virtue that made me feel comfortable talking with him. He always seemed to know when something was troubling me. In those days peer pressure was a major distraction in my life and Mr. Firebaugh had this innate ability to say the right thing at the appropriate moment.

I could not play sports because my father would not allow us. In order to get attention I acted out my frustration in the classrooms. Consequently, I began, just as in the early days, to get into a lot of trouble. Mr. Firebaugh and Ms. Lane were seemingly the only people who recognized what I was experiencing. Mr. Firebaugh would always tell me that I did not have to be an athlete to excel in school, and I did not have to be the class clown to get attention. He was the first instructor who actually made me feel smart and instilled in me a sense of self-esteem that has stuck with me until this very day.

Fairfield Junior High was full of a lot of new students that I did not know. Arnie was dating this older student named John. We had agreed to always remain friends, but whenever I saw her and him together I felt as if I was missing out on something. It is true what they say, that one never gets over their first love. Even to this very day I wonder how my life might have been different had our relationship been able to grow as we were growing.

Fairfield was just like Central Gardens School in that I was always being compared by teachers to my older siblings, who were all very disciplined and had left a legacy of being "goodie two shoes." A legacy that made it very difficult for me and shoes that I could not fit. I know they did not intend to do this but it sort of turned out that way.

My father was a heavy smoker and made us light his cigarettes often. As I look back I am sure this was an indirect cause of my early smoking—along with peer pressure of course. I began to hang with the in crowd, and the in crowd would always get me into trouble. We began to experience drugs, alcohol and sex. This was the beginning of a stifling trend that would stay with me for many years to come.

During those formative years we really began to care how we looked. No longer would I allow my mother to just go in a store and pick out my clothes. I wanted to go with her. Regardless of my desires she still only bought the things that she wanted to buy. My parents basically controlled every aspect of our lives. They were overly protective and my siblings were always concerned with pleasing them. However I had this strong desire to be different and I was—in most ways. After school I used to come home to my paper route, as that was the only way I could get out of the house. One day this popular girl named Kim that I liked was having a party. However since my parents did not allow us to attend these functions I did not bother to ask. So I told my parents that I was going out on my paper route to collect but instead I went to the party and lost track of time. My father came looking for me and thanks to my brother, he seemed to know exactly where I was and yelled at me to come home—which I did. When I got there he met me with an extension cord. I got a whipping that night and the entire neighborhood knew about it the next morning. The kids teased me at school about hearing my yelling and screaming. Those whippings I received never deterred me from doing what it was that got me the whippings in the first place. The elders would call this having a hard head. My father should have punished me for disobeying him. He should have talked to me about the consequences of not obeying and what could happen because of my disobedience. Personally I now feel that type of punishment is useless and should be deemed obsolete.

About mid-way through my second year at Fairfield Junior High my family moved to a new home in the posh Dabbs House District, not too far from Central Gardens. To move in that neighborhood was considered to be a prodigal leap up in the social class.

CHAPTER TWO

DADDY'S WISH

As far back as I can remember we had attended Cedar Street Memorial Baptist Church. My mother had been a member there even before Cynthia was born. We were all baptized by the Reverend Dr. Benjamin William Robertson who was the son of a minister and, in my biased opinion, one of the most effective spiritual orators I have ever witnessed. My siblings and I had to attend Sunday school every week. I did not understand exactly why we always had to go there; however, my mother was extremely adamant about having complete control over that aspect of our lives. After Sunday school we would take turns saving my mother a seat near the front of the sanctuary.

She was radically zealous about sitting in that seat. Some days two of us had to do this because occasionally my father would attend. However, mom would be there every Sunday. When I was delegated to save the seat she made me sit there with her. I was relatively young then and frequently fell asleep with my head on her lap.

I have many memories of Cedar Street Memorial Baptist Church; in fact most of our socializing was done there. Since we were unable to play with the kids in the neighborhood, we were well known amid the congregational community. There were a lot of child members of that church. Most of us came from similar backgrounds so we all had a lot in common. Aside from what was taught to us in Sunday school we had limited knowledge of the doctrinal affairs of the church. However Rev. Dr. Robertson is a charismatic preacher and kept that church full to capacity every Sunday. In looking back at those worship services in Cedar Street Memorial Baptist Church, I can truthfully affirm that those experiences have had a reverberating effect on me. My siblings and I were introduced to Christ at an early age and this gave us an incredible head start on life. In my opinion everyone should be inaugurated to God while still young. Surely the godliness of parents is passed on in covenant to the children, and those children continue to touch the world with healing.

My first year at Highland Springs High School was an unpleasant adventure. It was 1976 and there were many distractions in my life that had little to do with school. Vices had begun to take dominion in my life and I was no longer certain of my destiny. I was smoking pot and drinking alcohol. My father had begun to exhibit signs of chronic alcoholism. He was going in and out of the hospital with significant frequency. Each time that he was admitted the diagnosis and medication would be more potent. I remember all the doctors telling him time and time again that if he did not stop drinking alcohol eventually he would die. He had lost his job as the sexton at a church on the fashionable west end of town just before we moved from Central Gardens, apparently because of the huge amount of time that he was spending in the hospitals.

Since I had been thrown out of Highland Springs High School by my second year, my father and I were spending a lot of time together. He had become successful in the wholesale seafood business and we would sell fresh seafood straight off the truck. This was extremely profitable and I was making more money than I had previously ever made in my entire life. My father and I had many touching conversations while working out of that truck. He told me that he would not be living much longer and I believe he had begun to express himself sentimentally. The apostle Paul wrote in his second epistle to the Church in Corinth, "For while we are in this tent, we groan and are burdened, because we do not wish to be clothed but to be clothed with our heavenly dwelling, so that what is normal may be swallowed up by life" (2 Corinthians 5:4).

My parents were like many African-American parents in that they did not love us equally. However I do believe they loved us adequately. There were no disputes amongst my siblings and me; we all knew that my brother Junie was the charm of my father's heart. Subconsciously I may have questioned my father's love for my sisters and me until those moments when he expressed his sensitivity. Fortunately for me, we shared those moments of expression—otherwise we may have never had the opportunity to know each other as we really were. Up until those moments, I do not believe we ever really knew each other. Moreover, and equally important, he was a very wise man and revealed a verity that later came to pass. He said after he had died my life would be very different. I did not know exactly what he meant by this. However in the years ahead, this revelation that my father had proved to be true.

In mid-July 1978, when I was sixteen years old, I was sentenced to thirty days in Juvenile Hall because of an altercation that I had had with my sister Cynthia over the telephone. I was on the phone one night and she wanted to use it. When I did not get off of the phone at her request, she came into my room with a bat. I took the bat and when she tried to hit me with her fist—I beat her up. She called the police, I was arrested. This was the first experience that my family had with incarceration, which was basically incomprehensible to them. My parents came to see me sometime at the end of that month. Apparently the entire family was going on a vacation for a week and they wanted to visit before they left. I assured them that I would be fine but I needed some money. Daddy, who had a tendency to be generous, reached in his pocket and pulled out some quarters, then threw them on the table. I told them as they were leaving, "good-bye mom, good-bye dad." That was the last time I saw my father alive.

On August 10, 1978 I experienced a spiritual phenomenon. An Angel revealed to me in a dream that my earthly father had been taken and that I would surmount this tragedy. The next morning the Assistant Director of Juvenile Hall came into my cell with this somber look on his face and said he regrettably was the bearer of bad news. In perturbation I responded to his comment by saying that my father was dead. He glanced at me with a look of amazement and asked if I had a dream? Surreally I confirmed his inquiry. He assured me that I would be immediately released and that my brother would be picking me up within the hour. Suddenly I began to weep, unlike I had ever wept in my entire life. The Assistant Director embraced me with compassion, holding me until a worker came to inform us that my brother had arrived.

On the way home my brother and I began to contemplate our future. In a brief moment our entire lives had changed. The person we knew as dad was no more. The intensely stringent man that we had proclaimed many times we hated was gone. Suddenly all we could do was shed tears of love, loneliness and abandonment. We knew a part of us had died along with him. The boys that he left on earth instantly became men. We knew there were many tests and trials we would have to endure. Our parents were so important in our lives and now one of them was gone forever. Thoughts of what my father had told me during those days we spent in that truck immediately came to mind. This proved to be the most significant period I had ever experienced in my brief life.

Daddy's demise was difficult for all of us. He was the brother his sisters looked to for inspiration. He was the son his parents looked to for assurance. He was the dad we depended on as a crutch. He was the husband my mother looked to for companionship and guidance—in many ways all of our lives changed. His funeral was prompt and very personal and he was buried under a tree that he loved on my mother's property.

My mother was a young, vibrant, beautiful thirty-eight year old. Since she had left most of the raising of the kids, especially the disciplining, to my father, we expected minimal change around the household. I believed she wanted to relinquish her responsibility as a rearing parent after my father's transition. Sandra had married Comer a year earlier and had already moved out of the house. Cynthia had already left for Radford College, so mom, Junie and I were the only three in the household.

Instantly I began to observe what my father had forewarned me regarding change. As for the parenting and the disciplining it was a mandate of the past. Suddenly after those years of strict guidance and protection, we found ourselves able to do anything we wanted. I had begun to work for Carroll Epps more often. His son Malcolm and I had been best friends for as far back as I could remember. We would "spin records" at functions in the greater Richmond metropolitan area. Actually we had been doing that since we were fourteen years old. My parents allowed it because I was making good money and Carroll was a very likable person with good morals. After the passing of my father I became more involved in the operations of Carroll's business. The important things such as family, school and church became trivial. It became obvious that I had become a man. School and everything about it no longer interested me. Girls my age did not interest me either. Especially since I had begun to spend a lot of time with Margarite who was ten years older and taught me a lot about life in general. Besides she was totally in tune with my sexuality. I had become a man and she was the first woman who treated me as such.

During that period I noticed my destiny taking control and knew my school days were limited, despite the pleas from my mother to remain involved in school. Since I had been expelled from Highland Springs High School permanently, I had to attend Henrico High where I unyieldingly did not want to go. Ms. West, a scrupulous teacher there, and my mother were the only people who never gave up on me. Until those days in October 1979, when everything else and all the odds were against me, Ms. West was still insisting there was something special about me. She continued to reinforce what I now believe my mother was trying to do and just could not find the words to simply say "Continue your education!" I thanked Ms. West for all that she had done for me, however, that tumultuous voyage had come to an end. Despite the pain, disgrace and dismay that I would cause to everyone associated with me, especially my family, I walked out of Ms. West's classroom, never to return to high school again.

Meanwhile there were still these vices, augmented by drugs and constant drinking, that had taken precedence in my life. There were court appearances all over the county. Since I was still only seventeen years old my problems were also my mother's problems. I had come to the conclusion that I had begun to cause my family too much stress and pain. A judge gave me an ultimatum to leave Richmond, or go to jail. On November 21, 1979 I left Richmond, Virginia and to this very day I can count on one hand the amount of times that I have gone back there.

CHAPTER THREE

ALARM IN MY HEAD

A lot of what happened to me during those years of wandering was a direct result of being so young and on my own. During the early 1980s, survival dictated all of my actions. My life had become so intense that there was little time to identify with my past. I had a distorted impression of myself and no sense of direction, lacking goals. I was extremely conscious of my surroundings because there were wolves out there. 1 Peter 5:8 tells us, "Be self controlled and alert. Your enemy the devil prowls around like a roaring lion looking for someone to devour." Actually I knew that God was protecting me, although I felt that thanking and praising Him would be a testament of the weaknesses that I was so afraid of acknowledging. My Bible was something I would keep around and look at from time to time.

There were many cities in the United States that became temporary homes for me; however I found concord and tranquility in Monterey, California. This was an Army town and most people there were from someplace else, which took away my feelings of being a misfit. Since there were many people in this vacation resort and military community, I could easily survive off the environment. Making money came naturally to me and I seemed to always have a lot of it.

Just as it had been when I was growing up in Richmond, I could not seem to discard the negative people around me. These groupies seemed to be legitimate and sincere; however, there was always something deep inside of me that made me feel uncomfortable whenever they were around. Rather than telling them to get lost I turned to alcohol and drugs to pacify those uncomfortable urges.

In essence I was becoming an alcoholic and a drug addict and most of the undesirable people around me used drugs and alcohol too, so this problem escalated. My consumption of these drugs and alcohol escalated also. Whenever I came down from these "highs" there was this Voice inside my head telling me to stop, but I wouldn't. This Voice was telling me that I was doing things that I did not want to do. The apostle Paul wrote to the Romans, "I know that nothing good lives in me, that is, in my sinful nature. For I have the desire to do what is good, but I cannot carry it out. For what I do is not the good I want to do; no, the evil I do not want to do, this I keep on doing. Now if I do what I do not want to do, it is no longer I who do it, but it is sin living in me that does it" (Romans 7:18).

Suddenly I started to feel inadequate about not completing my High School education, so I applied for the GED Examination through an adult school. There was little doubt that I could pass that test. So, in February 1980 I took the GED Examination and passed it on my first attempt. Now, as least when I filled out an application I could put down that I had a High School diploma. The success of passing that test made me hunger deep down inside for more knowledge. That Voice inside my conscience became louder and manifested into strength, drive and ambition. Suddenly my destiny was becoming distinctively clearer.

Subsequently, I saw an ad about a Community College that read, "You can enroll, if you have a GED," and that financial aid was available. This set an alarm off in my head since financial aid meant money. I had scored high on my SAT examination when I was in the ninth grade, so when I applied to Monterey Peninsula College I was immediately accepted.

When I started MPC my intention was not to get a degree, it was just to collect the financial aid. This became a means of survival for me, and that means became a way of life. There was nothing more important to me than that campus. I became extremely familiar with how all of that financial aid bureaucracy functioned and since I was a recipient of work-study, I was required to get a job. My skills were somewhat limited so my choices were too. However, there was a positive quality that I had acquired from my street knowledge and that was the ability to effectively communicate. My EOP counselor told me about an opening in the Student Activities Office for an Assistant Student Coordinator. I went there and met a man named Mel. Later I met Mel's supervisor, Robert, and those two men would ultimately change the direction of my entire existence. There were a few persons that had left lasting impressions on my life, but until that point, none had touched my life so profoundly. Instantly, knowledge, which has always intrigued me, was profusely available and almost autonomously I became aware that I was not even the person that I thought I was.

Mel and Robert were in many ways complete opposites, although they seemed to have similar thinking patterns. Mel, however, was an extremely politically-minded individual and he was very active in African awareness, women's rights, Student Affairs and the Socialist movements. Whenever there was a controversial issue in the community, Mel and his followers were there. Mel was the Student Activities Coordinator, so obviously the political fervor amongst the students at MPC was intense. One night my friends and I were stopped by the Seaside Police Department because of what they called "erratic driving." In our opinion it was harassment and a scuffle between the police and ourselves ensued. The police got hurt; however, we were not the aggressors and also got hurt a bit. There was a drunk-driving charge that was later dropped due to, in my opinion, a press conference held by my friends and me regarding the police harassment of African-American males, which was so prevalent in the community in the early 80s. Mel and some other members of his political party attended that press conference in our support and were extremely active in the observations of the day.

Mel taught me some self-control. Since I was only eighteen years old when we met, I assume there were many rough edges that needed to be smoothed out. He imparted to me wisdom about an establishment that was not conducive for young African-American males trying to survive independently. He also provided me with a network of other politically active people such as I had become. He made me realize that I could achieve goals independently and set a standard for younger males to strive to attain. I can uprightly vouch that Mel is a role model and I know that I was blessed to have had the opportunity to be acquainted with him.

Robert was also vivaciously encompassed in the development of my somewhat lead academic tenure. Robert was everything that I had envisioned myself to be in the future. He was bountifully educated and possessed a certain ambience about himself that was desirous to say the least. All the young black men at that school, that I knew, wanted to be like him. His title was that of Assistant Dean of Student Activities and he seemed to always be in control of himself. He was the best communicator that I had ever met. Contrary to Mel, who appeared to always be in the limelight, Robert was more laid back and sort of let life come to him. I am not sure if he was aware that I was in constant observation of his every move. Since he was aware of my storied past he sort of took me under his wing, so to speak, and did not allow me enough rope to hang myself.

During those years he was the authoritative person in my life; unlike the "Big Brother" image that Mel was providing me, Robert came just short of the father figure. He never ceased to tell me what to do and what not to do, all the while knowing that I was still in a rebellious stage left from my childhood. Robert was the first person I was inclined to accept direction from. Deep inside I had a trust in him that superseded that trust that I had had for those teachers in my youth. I believed what he told me, and knew that my welfare was important to him. He would not tell me anything that would prove detrimental and this made it easier to accept his direction. Since he was a living example of what I considered success then, it was understandable for any young man to want to be like him.

Robert, just like Mel, was extremely political. Since I was only eighteen years old I wanted to be like them, I wanted and needed to be political. Subsequently, I ran for and won a seat on the Monterey Peninsula Community College Board of Trustees as the student representative and Robert was the administrative advisor to the position. So, in essence he was my boss, my advisor and had become my friend and confidant. There were many times when my life became overwhelmed and Robert seemed to always have the needed advice. As I look back at those years, I know that God brings people into others' lives for specific purposes and I continue to thank Him for bringing Mel and Robert into mine.

Bonnie, who was Robert's secretary, also brought direction and I can remember her always telling me that I could make it on my own if I concentrated on goals and strove to perfect myself. Joshua 1:2 tells us, "I will give you every place where you set your foot, as I promised Moses." She was the epitome of an authentic parent. Everything about Bonnie had this motherly mysticism attached to it. I believe Bonnie, in many ways, considered me to be her surrogate son and treated me as such. Then, I could not appreciate those motherly traits; now that I am older I understand what it was that she was doing.

Although the Student Activities Office provided me with collective wisdom there was a definite mutual exclusiveness about those three. Yet, there was also a mutual inclusiveness in terms that they all seemed to have a common goal where I was concerned—they all were determined to touch my life so prodigally by way of intelligence, caring and compassion.

Although Monterey Peninsula College had taken dominion of my life in the daytime, there was still this adversary that had control of my life at night. Greta and Niecy were two young ladies who had been close friends of mine since I had moved to California. We all were inseparable and did everything together from going to the clubs, to driving the northern coast of California. Although Niecy was my girlfriend, she was married. Her husband lived in Germany and was in the Army. So our relationship could have been considered an affair. Moses wrote in Leviticus 20:10, "If a man commits adultery with another man's wife, with the wife of his neighbor, both the adulterer and the adulteress must be put to death." Thank God that Jesus granted us clemency for this sin in John 8:10, when he said to the woman that the Pharisees had brought him after she had been caught committing adultery, "Woman, where are they? Has no one condemned you?" "No one, sir," she said. "Then neither do I condemn you," Jesus declared. "Go now and leave your life of sin." Strangely, it all seemed very normal to us during that time. None of us had God in our lives then so we all were sort of just existing.

During the first year of our relationship Niecy was summoned to Germany to be with her husband. Since we were so close and spent so much of our time together the separation was difficult. However, we knew her departure was inevitable and we had prepared ourselves for it. We expressed our love for each other in a final unreserved manner and gracefully parted company. Although we did not know if we would ever see each other again, I do believe we both felt a sense of security in having had the opportunity to experience the freedom we found in our sinful relationship.

Greta became my girlfriend after Niecy left and for some reason I assumed it was the natural thing to do. There was never

VOICES OF MY FATHER

a doubt in our minds that we were attracted to each other. We all knew that Niecy was married and eventually would be leaving so I believe this must have been lingering on her mind. Greta and I seemed to communicate with each other with benevolence. She knew most of my thoughts and since we were so close friends for a long period of time we were tolerant of other people being in our lives. In looking back at our relationship I realized for the first time that the "friends first" philosophy does work and would recommend it for everyone.

Greta and Niecy were extremely gifted at making money. My friend Ross, from Atlanta, and I would give them each one hundred marijuana joints every night, then drop them off at the club, pick them up after the club closed, and each would have at least two hundred dollars. This became a way of life for us and provided us with financial security. Ross was a very streetwise quick thinker. He was a army specialist who drank all the time and seem never to be far away from wherever I was.

After Niecy moved, Greta had to find a new home since she had been living with Niecy's family. This was part of their prior agreement and also the start of a new chapter in my life. She moved in with her older sister Jean, who I only knew cordially in passing, sometimes giving her a ride places. But I had begun to spend a great deal of time at Jean's house because of Greta. And although Greta and I liked to spend a lot of time together I had grown weary of going to the clubs every night and had decided to take a break. So after I had dropped her off at the nightclub I would go back over to Jean's house where she and I would have drinks. One night one thing led to another and we became sexually intimate.

Jean eventually put Greta out after informing her of our

intentions to live together. This was the first time I had experienced this, and even though it was a serious matter I was flattered by what was transpiring. However there was always, just as it had been when I was a boy, some Voice telling me this lifestyle that I was falling in love with was not right. Add this to my daytime environment, which kept some balance in my life, and it made life rather confusing.

Along with Jean came cocaine, lots of it. The marijuana that I had become so accustomed to, no longer interested me. Cocaine was now the drug of choice and with it brought a sense of prestige. Since I knew how to make big money I could afford it and we were having some lavish parties. There continued to always be many people around me and we were all doing the same things. My friends at school were also undercover drug addicts and we progressed from snorting to smoking it in an extremely short period of time. My name became synonymous with cocaine. I would snort it in the mornings before I went to class, snort it before a test and snort it after a test. Since we used to sell a lot of it we could support our own and other people's habits. The names may have changed but the game was still the same.

Everything seemed to go to another level with Jean. She had been a prostitute in her teenage years and was not reserved about going out there and making money if we needed it. I was fortunate because there were many times that the opportunity presented itself for me to use drugs intravenously; however that Voice did not allow me to try it. Honestly I must admit that I was afraid to do it.

With Jean there came fights and arguments, more than I was accustomed to and, in time this became inconducive to my lifestyle. There was literally a harem of women constantly around me and I subsequently began to pursue the type of women that were more in tune with my daytime life. I remember Weeda, from Omaha, who came to live with her sister down the hall from us. She was the most beautiful girl I had ever seen in my life—since Arnie. She had idiosyncrasies and features similar to Arnie, and I believed at that time it was love at first sight. Since the drugs and alcohol were deteriorating my relationship with Jean—our separation was imminent. I had begun to spend my time with Weeda, for she represented a way out of an alliance that I knew would eventually cause my untimely demise. While Jean lay at home passed out from the drugs and alcohol, Weeda and I were down the hall falling deeply in love. She was extremely young and naïve about the wickedness that the secular world was offering. Yet she intrigued me, and since Robert and Mel used to tell me all the time that this was the type of woman I needed I had begun to anxiously woo her.

Weeda and I became close and began to conspire how I was going to get out of the fiasco with Jean. We both knew this would not be easy and there would be problems ahead. However I do believe she had prepared herself and was earnestly waiting for me to make that move. Unknowingly I suddenly had become torn between two lovers. Realizing my dilemma I knew that I would eventually have to make a decision and I knew what that decision needed to be. However I could not make the only decision that would have made any sense in this love triangle.

There I was, locked in a relationship with a woman who had provided me with such security for a long time, while being in love with another. Since there was so much arguing, jealousy, mental and verbal abusing going on in my attachment with Jean the choice was not a hard one to make. I seemed to have confused emotions of guilt, security, love and infatuation that ultimately played a major part in my distorted drug-induced decision-making. Since I could not make the decision myself, Jean made it for everyone involved, once she found out I was seeing Weeda. She immediately went down to Weeda's sister's house and basically threatened to make everybody's lives extremely chaotic. My heart was with Weeda and her family and since I was aware of what Jean was capable of doing I could not in good conscience allow this situation to get any worse. As I look back at that situation, as I have done countless times, Weeda and I should have just left that area and started over some place else.

Eventually the inevitable happened when I returned home one day to find Jean engaged in a licentious act, causing us to ultimately go our separate ways. Paul wrote to the saints in Ephesus, "Having lost all sensitivity, they have given themselves over to sensuality so as to indulge in every kind of impurity, with a continual lust for more" (Ephesians 4:19). I had never experienced that kind of betrayal before and have not since. Her actions were motivated out of spite and it was a very contemptuous, bitter separation. There have been a significant number of women in my life and I have never really been able to sustain a long relationship. However, Jean is the only woman that when I left, I felt that I was permanently scarred. Hopefully, one day I will realize that is not the case.

In late 1981 after Jean and I separated, and a new era took dominion of my life. She had provided me with stability in my living situation, so I now found myself having to pay my way through life. It was not difficult, and just the idea that I had to do it proved to be an experience that I welcomed. Up until that point I had always made a lot of money and wasted it. Now, at least, I was afforded an opportunity to see where my money was going which gave me an added sense of responsibility.

Even with all that was going on in my life I had continued to attend MPC, as I was sure MPC would continue to provide me with income and knowledge. However since I had been released from the burden that Jean had placed on me, I immediately began to focus more on the important issues, such as my education and the people on campus that were becoming more intriguing by the day.

CHAPTER FOUR

REMEMBERING RHONDA

Once I had decided to major in business I began taking accounting classes. I was not remotely interested in accounting and was only taking the courses to fulfill a requirement. I met this girl in one of those classes named Rhonda, who was abundantly gifted intellectually. She was the only daughter in a very popular and influential family in the community. I wanted to get to know her because she was smart, and since I had begun to take the more difficult classes I felt that I should befriend her because she could make my situation more manageable—especially considering my night life.

However I felt that Rhonda would not like a guy such as

me. She and her family seemed so cultured and the presence of a streetwise person, such as myself, might make them uncomfortable or embarrassed. I was wrong and Rhonda did take a fancy towards me, a rather significant liking, and surprisingly her family did too. She was so much unlike the women that I had become accustomed to. She was younger than me, articulate, bright and well mannered. She had a personality such that in talking with her instantly you knew that she was going to be successful. Moreover and equally important she was a devout Christian, who believed in the sanctity of marriage and was determined to save her virginity for her husband. This immediately presented a challenge for me. Rhonda always proclaimed that she could hold out on sex until marriage. Since I was a strong-willed young man who usually got what I wanted, this quest became a prodigious undertaking.

Rhonda became more to me than a quest, she became a friend, a confidant and her environment became refuge for me. She was the first person I had ever met that made me wish that I could turn back the hands of time. Once again I found myself infatuated with a innocent girl who was so much different than me. Any young man would be proud to call her his own and I knew that I had better enjoy her while I had the opportunity. My buddies, "Big James" and "Johnny B," always told me that she was different than any other girl that I had ever known. They said that I should treat her with ingenious care and I did. They did not know this at the time but I was still suffering inside from the scars left by my relationship with Jean. After all I was still only twenty years old and my concentration was somewhat blurred. Her family, sensing the robust distress deep within my soul, adamantly attempted to embrace me and continued to invite me to their church. Although that Voice inside of me constantly told me to accept their invitations, the flesh outside would not allow me to expose my vulnerabilities and subsequently I passed up those opportunities. I was not yet ready to make a gallant effort to escape the lifestyle that I knew would eventually destroy me. Rhonda and I spoke often of spending the rest of our lives together. But somehow for some reason I never really thought that would actualize. I knew I was not prepared, and all this appeared too good to be true.

One night Big James and I were en route to a New Years' Eve party at Rhonda's. We had been heavily drinking, as usual, before the party, because we knew that since we were not yet 21 years old her parents would forbid us to drink alcohol at their house. I fell asleep at the wheel of my car, running a red light and violently smashing into another car in the intersection. Amazingly, although both cars were totaled, nobody got hurt. The police arrived and luckily the officer knew me because I worked with his wife at MPC and he let us go. He could have easily charged me with reckless drunk driving and put both of us in jail. However, he didn't and we jumped into the back of a passing truck driven by a friend, requesting to be dropped off at Rhonda's house.

Although I had escaped another brush with death it seemed that there was a definitive message in all of this. There we were about to enter our fantasy world once again and our lives flashed before us. We went to that New Year's Eve party and had fun as if nothing had ever happened, not telling anyone of our recent brush with mortality.

Rhonda graduated from MPC that spring and all of a sudden I started to feel somewhat lonely. I believe that her graduation afforded me an opportunity to examine my own situation in terms of possibly transferring to the University system. Rhonda's parents had this godliness about them, as did mine, affording her a head start on life. Her dreams were manifesting themselves right before our very eyes. There was little to ponder in terms of her immediate future after graduating from Junior College. She would be transferring to the University system in the fall.

Since I had grown to legitimately love Rhonda and her family, I did not know what to expect in terms of her leaving. She had decided to attend California State University at Fresno and received her acceptance letter rather late. However it was conclusive that Rhonda would be attending that University in the fall and majoring in Journalism.

I was extremely proud of Rhonda and wanted only the best for her. A part of me wanted to accompany her, but it was evident from her enthusiasm about leaving home and venturing into the unknown that this was something she had to do alone. Affectionately I understood because I had had those same feelings before and could vividly remember them. In that brief instant she became my role model and I knew that someday I too would transfer to the University system.

Early one fall morning, Rhonda's family and I loaded up the car and drove her to Fresno. Upon arriving where she would spend the first semester in the co-ed dorms, I could feel her excitement. I could see in her eyes the confusion between joyful anticipation and the emotional certainty that she would be leaving her family. I believed she could deal with leaving me because of the newness of her environment and the people she would meet. Deep down I knew our days as an item were numbered. Better still, my love for her had grown unconditionally, and I was willing to part with this young person who had unknowingly healed some of those scars, for the sake of her finding her niche in this complicated world.

Rhonda kissed me passionately and told me that she would always love me, then her family and I left Fresno. As we were driving back to Monterey I felt a sense of abandonment. With all the alienation I have experienced in my life I still had never been attached to a family the way I was attached to hers. I knew that my separation from Rhonda would also mean the separation of her family from me, and this would mean drawing closer to the very vices I had been running from. Since I had been staying with Big James and his family on Fort Ord, I suddenly found myself spending more time with them. MPC still was my source of survival, but it just wasn't the same once Rhonda had left.

Despite the constant appeals from Mel, Robert and Bonnie, I found myself slipping more and more back into a lifestyle that I so zealously wanted to leave. Getting high with Big James, Johnny B and Champ became my pastime. Virgil and Carolyn, both moms that had to go to school as a condition of receiving aid, had joined our clan and each contributed quite generously to our already expensive and expanded cocaine habits. In those days we would meet up at school just to jump in our cars and drive to the beach to compare the quality and quantity of the drugs each of us had. We would get high, then go to class and try to pass a test. We were fooling ourselves into thinking those drugs made us smarter. Somehow I seemed to be the one who barely passed so we continued our lives as respectable alcoholics and drug addicts—by the way, we were all very much functional. Paul wrote in 1 Corinthians 5:11, "But now I am writing you that you must not associate with anyone who calls himself a brother but is sexually immoral or greedy, an idolater or a slanderer, a drunkard or a swindler. With such a man, do not even eat."

One day in mid 1982 Big James's family asked me to move out and I did—to Seaside with another friend Sam Brown. He was a disc jockey and since I had been one myself during my childhood days with Malcolm and his dad, I immediately viewed this as an opportunity to put some more money in my pocket. Sam and I also had something else very significant in common. Some people felt that we looked so much alike that they could not tell us apart. Both of us were extremely popular personalities in the community and we had a concubine following us around wherever we went.

Since some people could not tell us apart, we would sometimes pretend to be each other in order to trick some girls. This worked out fine most times since we both had more women than we could manage. Sam was actually living with his girlfriend Denise, and in essence I was living with her too. Both of us made a lot of money, even opening up a record store at one point. We were extremely good friends and I believe some of those good traits that I had leftover from childhood rubbed off on him. Sam also was interested in Edith, who was another one of Jean's sisters. Although Jean and I were no longer together I still visited her frequently.

It seemed as though we spent a relatively small, yet significant amount of time over there. I felt somewhat uncomfortable at times, but since Sam was doing all that he could in order for me to stay at Denise's house I felt obligated to assist him in this minute way. Jean knew I was just there to accommodate my trusted and good friend. I believe she and I had come to a point where we could exercise civil behavior in the same room. Sam and I always had drugs wherever we went and those drugs carried a certain measure of respect. Unfortunately we were unaware that this respect came at a high price. Eventually Denise got fed up with Sam and put both of us out. I do not believe that this mutinous disposition was the direct result of anything that we had done. After all, we did contribute quite generously to the household expenses.

Coincidentally, just as I had recently experienced with Jean, the womanizing was a bit more than Denise could tolerate. I understood completely what Sam was going through but I could not help him much because suddenly he could not help me and we both found ourselves homeless. Jeremiah warned us when he wrote in Lamentations 4:5, "Those who once ate delicacies are destitute in the street. Those nurtured in purple now lie on ash heaps." I had been there before and once again relied on my network which was firmly established from my associations at MPC. Sam, on the other hand, had to rely on his reputation as someone who always had drugs and moved in with Johnny B, who was more than accommodating even through he was renting from an elderly woman.

In late 1982 I moved in with Watts, who I knew from my days with Niecy. He was Niecy's oldest sister Tally's boyfriend. He was also attending MPC part-time and was a full time Correctional Officer at Soledad State Prison. Because of his high-paying profession, Watts was financially secure and lived well. He was a good person as he had been raised to be. He had a strong sense of right and wrong, good and evil. Watts was a native of Gainesville, Florida, so he, just like all of my other circle of undesirables, did not have family in the immediate area.

We were like brothers and this seem to substitute that void of not belonging to a family. Both of us were thousands of miles away from home. Watts also had serious drug and drinking problems, and often brought the stress of his job home with him. Our schedules were different so we never saw each other much, which was convenient considering the nature of our relationship. Often Watts would have temper tantrums when certain friends of mine would stop over. He felt most of them were drug addicts and he was right most of the time, so whenever he was home I used to limit my company out of respect for him. One day Dirty Thirty, from Memphis, and Hollywood, from Kansas City, stopped over and Hollywood went to the back of the apartment for a significant period of time. I thought maybe he was in the bathroom, however I found out later that he had stolen Watt's diamond ring. This was devastating in terms of Watts and my living arrangements and eventually, after numerous arguments, I moved out.

Jacko, who was an elderly German man with a lot of history in the Monterey community, rented me a room. He was retired and living in a condominium on Hillcrest. His company owned the entire block of condos and he had so much money that he spent a significant amount of time out of the country. Jacko had one rule—he prohibited drinking alcohol in his house. He did not mind me eating his food and he did not even mind if I was late a couple weeks on the rent. He was a recovering alcoholic and did not want any alcohol around his house.

I could abide this small rule because he was gone most of the time, then I could drink as much as I wanted and he never knew about it. Jacko understood that I was young and was extremely impressionable in a lot of ways. He sensed this and eloquently enlightened me about a world that I knew nothing about. He spoke several languages fluently and up until that point in my life I had yet to meet anyone who had traveled the world. Jacko seemed to have a handle on life, much like Robert and Mel. He knew the mistakes that he had made in his past and why he had made them. He was adamant about not making the same mistakes and even though he was white and I was black, I always felt a sense of Agape love—unconditional love for him. It was as if he allowed me to make mistakes only to tell me what I might have done wrong. Jacko was also a self-proclaimed mathematician and helped me with my Algebra. I learned to appreciate math because of him.

Living at Jacko's also afforded me a higher standard of living than I had previously been used to. Even though Watts' apartment was comfortable it couldn't compare to the eccentricity that Jacko's condo provided. The entire place was like my own and I would extravagantly live it up whenever he was not around. When he was home he asked me to make myself scarce because he too was quite debonair in his own right and also a ladies' man. I could relate to this and respected his wishes.

One night after excessive partying with my friends I came home extremely drunk, put some food on the stove, and fell asleep only to be wakened by Jacko, the entire condo full of smoke. The pan on the stove had caught fire and by the grace of God, Jacko came home and actually saved my life. However, this was an indication to him that I violated the only rule that he stringently mandated. He knew now that there was indeed an alcoholic in the house. It was also the first time I felt there may indeed be a problem in my life with this dreaded disease. Nevertheless, this gave Jacko the leverage to request that I move.

Since it was evident that I had violated his only rule, I respected his wishes, although once again I found myself seeking a place to live.

Almost instantly I moved in with another rather elderly wealthy individual. However, this one was of Irish descent and female. I was not sure at the time why all of these older people of another race were taking me in. Could it be they were seeking absolution from a sense of quilt for something that their ancestors had done? Or, were they Angels of the Lord entertaining strangers? The writer of Hebrews reminded us of this in 13:2, "Do not forget to entertain strangers, for by so doing some people have entertained angels without knowing it." I didn't ask many questions and since they were helping me out I really couldn't. All I knew was that they all seemed to like and trust me.

Darlie was a charming person and went to church twice a week. She was the only other person since Rhonda's family that invited me to church. Hebrews 1:14 tells us, "Are not all angels ministering spirits sent to serve those who will inherit salvation?" I didn't accept her invitations either, not necessarily because I didn't want to go to church, but because I could use that time when she was away from home to kind of do my own thing. Darlie really appreciated the fact that I was in the house. I never really left the house much until she was asleep because it was located in the high crime district and I did not feel safe so I knew she did not either.

In her home was when I really began to appreciate the things that people would try to do or were doing for me. I am not sure why that life-long lesson came to me in Darlie's house, but that's where it was. I remember my brother Junie coming out to California and visiting the Monterey Peninsula. He stayed with me for a couple of days and since I had not seen him since Big Pa's funeral his presence made me happy at first. Although we had fun I got the sense that he was making a report on me to be delivered to my family when he returned home. I resented the fact that he was making judgments about my life and I was offended by the comments that he was making concerning my lifestyle. But still, Darlie was extremely sweet in making arrangements for his visit. After he left I remember saying to myself that it was not soon enough.

The Monterey Peninsula Community College Board to which I had been elected began to consume my time. There came many occasions when I had to go to a different part of the state to attend conventions. I remember Robert coming to pick me up so we could car pool to one in San Jose. This also presented an opportunity for me to observe Robert in the business world, up close and personal, and he knew that I was checking out his every move. He acted accordingly in an attempt to show me correct business etiquette, even down to attire. At San Jose, Robert kept a watchful eye on me. He was making sure that I was progressing in virtuous ways that would mold me into a versatile business person. He and Mel used to do this for me, no matter where and what we were doing.

Afterwards, Darlie would ask me about the progress I felt that I had made and what additional benefits the students of MPC may have gained because of my efforts. I found out later that she and Bonnie had talked about how I had become Robert's protégé; considering the distinguished reputation that he held in the world of academia this was the ultimate compliment.

In the meantime I had picked up another drunk driving ticket and had been sentenced to serve ninety days in an Alcoholic

Rehabilitation Program called SunStreet in Salinas, about twenty miles east of Monterey. But, I was given a stay of execution until I graduated from MPC in the spring. Since I was barely twenty-one years of age I was naïve to the judicial system and felt the Judge may have been too stern. Although, considering this was the second offense in a short period of time it may well have been what I needed. Still, I was not convinced of this and became resistant and sought ways out.

In the spring of 1983, when I was only twenty-one years old, just as the year before when Rhonda had graduated from MPC, I graduated too. There were a few classes that had to be made up, and I was aware that I would either have to return to MPC or have to go to another school to complete those general education classes. Since I was moving into SunStreet in Salinas I might as well enroll in Hartnell Community College which was located in that town.

After my brother's visit I was filled with nostalgia and melancholy while thinking of other days. I thought that I had totally dealt with this mused sentiment. In my indecisive meditation I heard that Voice again—this time instructing me to go home. In the summer of 1983, I went to the Welfare Department in Seaside and told them that I wanted to go home to Virginia but I did not have the money to get there. A Social Worker arranged for a Greyhound bus ticket. Moses told us in Genesis 31:3, "Then the Lord said to Jacob, Go back to the land of your fathers and to your relatives, and I will be with you." Late that summer I left Seaside not knowing if I would ever return on a cross-country journey. Just as in the past, this journey would ultimately change the world as I knew it, forever.

CHAPTER FIVE

GOING HOME

The distance between Seaside, California and Richmond, Virginia is roughly, 3800 miles. I was prepared to be on a bus for about 3 days. Donna, Dirty Thirty's wife, fried some chicken and made some sandwiches for my trip. The bus would be traveling the northern route across the United States, which was to be the first time, for me, traveling across the continent in the summer. There were some states we would go through that I had never visited before.

Something significant happened in Reno while we were at one of our many stops. A woman named Mandy boarded the bus and sat next to me. Since it was common to ask the passenger next to you their destination, I did. It turned out that Mandy was en route to Minneapolis. She was a recent widow in search of a new identity. In many ways Mandy and I shared a common bond, in that both of us were in search of ourselves. She needed security within herself because her husband had been the center of her universe. Although she was in her thirties I could sense this girlish enthusiasm about her. It was intriguing and very stimulating, to say the least, and I felt she was heaven sent because I was needing a friend at that moment.

Mandy was a beautiful woman who had this smile that turned me into mush. She was notably vulnerable and even mentioned that she had never been with any man sexually except her husband. When we arrived in Omaha she wanted to get a good night's sleep and asked if I would share a hotel suite with her. Under normal circumstances I would have obliged her wishes, especially since she insisted that she would pay for everything. But I wanted to press forward and continue my journey home. This displeased her somewhat, but she got back on the bus and continued toward her destination also.

Mandy and I talked a lot about God and His purpose for us and our destinies. We seemed to have a lot in common. Although the time that we spent together was something like a day and a half, we became very good friends and felt a little uneasy about parting in Chicago. Unfortunately, we rolled into the "Windy City" behind schedule and had very little time to say our good-byes. However, we kissed and ran to our respective connections, she going north to Minnesota, and I continued heading east toward Virginia. I was sort of glad that we parted in this way because we had grown somewhat attached to each other in a very short period of time.

Chicago represented the halfway point in my journey.

Feelings of anxiety and fear of the unknown began to encompass me. Since my family did not know I was coming home I was unsure of how they would react. I had been gone for four years and I knew things would be different. Although I didn't know how different. I knew that life had changed after my father passed and since I hadn't spent any time with my family I felt apprehensive about going home. Would my mother welcome me with open arms? No I really didn't think so! How would my brother Junie react? Not well I supposed! Yet I was sure Cynthia would not be glad to see me so I expected some resistance. All I knew was I missed them very much and hoped, in some minute way, the feeling would prove mutual. The closer the bus got to Richmond the more I thought about them. So much so, until it came to a point that this anxiety consumed my entire thoughts.

    The time came when we pulled up into the Greyhound station in Richmond. As in any case, when you return to a place after a long absence, everything seems smaller. We arrived in Richmond about mid-day in late August and I knew that there would be no one at my mother's house to let me in. So I called my favorite cousin Gail and asked her to come and pick me up and she did. We went back to her house and there I was greeted with opened arms by her father, my Uncle Tibby. He seemed somewhat relieved that I was back in Richmond. Uncle Tibby was a big man who was also suffering from the side effects left from serving tours of duty in Vietnam. My father and he were married to sisters and were really good friends, and although my father was unable to serve in Vietnam because he had failed his physical, he was rather sensitive to Veteran causes. My aunt Sic, my mother's sister, was also very happy to see me, in fact their entire family was.

    Gail took me home around five-thirty. All I knew was during

that five-minute drive home this anxiety encompassed me. My Father's voice kept reverberating, telling me that things would be much different for me now that he was gone. As Gail and I sat in the car in the driveway of my mother's house, I have this very vivid memory of my mother looking out the window with this very unpleasant look on her face almost as if she was saying "say it isn't true." Immediately, I knew deep in my heart that this was not a good idea. I knew that my worst fears had come to pass. And I knew, even though I had not made it in the house, that my days were limited in this environment. I am sure, unlike I believe my mother is to this very day, that those expressions on her face changed my entire life as I knew it. Suddenly, I knew exactly what it was that my father had been telling me just before his transition. It was apparent that he knew something that I did not.

Although when I was a child I used to get into a lot of trouble and did things that embarrassed my family, I had grown out of most of that and considered myself a man. In the apostle Paul's attempt to purify the Church in Corinth, he wrote, "When I was a child, I talked like a child, I thought like a child, I reasoned like a child. When I became a man, I put my childish ways behind me" (1 Corinthians 13:11). I did not want to cause my family any more pain or embarrassment. Being conscious of this I made a sincere effort to control what I was doing and even got a job rather quickly.

Almost immediately my stay there became very uncomfortable. With the exception of Sandra, my family went out of their way to make me feel this way. Cynthia was a big part of this formulating conspiracy. I had wondered if she had ever forgiven me for the fight that we had which caused my commitment to

Juvenile Hall. Obviously, she had not and made it clear that I was not welcome in, what I mistakenly perceived to be, my own home. Junie, on the other hand, was never there much and basically went along with everything that my mother and Cynthia told him. My mother was almost wanting me out of the house as soon as I got there and she seemed to be waiting for the opportunity which made me more determined not to give it to her.

I had started working for Best Products, which is a low-priced department store on the west side of Richmond. My family knew my hours and used the fact that I got off work at 10:30 P.M. as a tool against me. Unlike in the big cities where the public transportation runs all night, in Richmond buses stop running just about 10:30 P.M. Since we lived clear on the other side of town it was extremely difficult for me to get home. My family did not trust me enough to allow me to drive any of their many cars and was extremely candid and adamant about not picking me up at night. It was as if they were setting me up for failure. They knew that I was not going to be able to continue to get home from the west side late at night, and this was effecting my ability at work also. Since I was working sometimes 16 hour days because it was getting close to Christmas, I would just go to work and then go to a friend's house to sleep and start that vicious cycle all over again.

As Christmas approached I remember many nights coming home hungry, late at night. Since I was paying my mother $200.00 a month to stay there, I felt that I was entitled to, at least, a meal or two. Occasionally, I would ask her for something to eat and she would say that she did not cook anything that night and that nobody ate. Then, my brother would come in and she would welcome him with a plate of hot food that she had hidden under the stove. There were many occasions such as this and after awhile I went to my mother and asked her about this attitude she had towards me, and she said that my brother was different.

In December, Junie hosted a Christmas party and it seemed as though everyone was there. It was a nice party and I got an opportunity to see some people I had not seen in a long time. My brother had purchased an enormous amount of beer. It was impossible for us to drink all of that beer and we did not. But, there was something that all of that leftover beer came to symbolize. That Friday before the party I had been laid off of my job, because the Christmas rush season was completed and our services were no longer needed. When I got home and told my mother that I had been laid off her attitude went from tolerable to unbearable. We knew that my lay off status had been inevitable because that was the condition of my employment in the first place.

On Monday after my brother's party I remember drinking one of his fifty-plus leftover beers. My mother saw me drinking the beer and said that my brother was going to be mad that I drank one of his beers. I told her that I had over three hundred dollars in my pocket and I would be more than willing to pay for his beer if he wanted. I really did not think my brother would even notice that one of his beers was missing. Or, I felt that he would not mind even if he did notice. My brother came upstairs to my room and asked me whether I drank one of his beers. I acknowledged that I had and offered to replace it if he took me to the store. If not, I inquired whether he had change for a twenty dollar bill, so I could pay him for it. He said that he was not going to take me to the store and that he was not going to give me change for the twenty dollar bill. He demanded that I give him the twenty dollar bill for that 50 cent beer. It was 11:00 P.M. and about 5 degrees outside, with knee-deep snow, and the nearest store was about a mile from my mother's house. No one offered to take me there. My brother kept insisting that I give him the twenty dollars for that one beer I consumed. I refused and he hit me in the face with his fist.

Personally, I cannot hit any member of my family and it was evident that evil spirits were definitely present in that house that night. So my brother, realizing that I was not going to hit him back, jumped on me. I covered my face and just laid there in shock. I could hear Cynthia at the bottom of the steps yelling for me to get out. Then I heard my mother coming up the steps, and I thought that she was going to stop my brother from hitting me. Instead she brandished a .38 caliber revolver in her hand and pointed it to my temple, pulling the trigger back, and ordered me to get out immediately. I honestly felt that her intentions were to shoot me.

That baleful instance once again changed my entire life. All I heard after that was my father's voice telling me that things would be different for me once he's gone. Over and over again, ever since that night I kept hearing his voice. After my brother got off of me I began to call around for help and remember getting in touch with my childhood friend Earl. I asked him to come and pick me up. And he, did along with his little brother Buck, and a mutual childhood friend named Smoke, all of whom I had grown up with.

We went to an after-hour party that night and all got real drunk. I must have passed out because when I woke up I was on the front steps of my mother's house. I had taken all the money that I had with me that night, but I was broke and was not sure how I had gotten home. My mother let me in the house on her way to work and told me that we were going to talk when she came home.

When she returned I informed her that I had been "clipped" of all my money and was broke. She told me that I had to leave there and asked whether I wanted to go back to California. I said yes and she went on to offer to buy me a ticket back to California, which she did forthwith. I was to leave on Saturday which was fine with me because it was just after Christmas and right before the New Year. Everyone seemed to be glad that I was leaving again, with the exception of Sandra who never really had understood just what was happening around that house. Since I really never talked much to any of them she only had to go on what my family was saying.

Since my bus was leaving at 6:00P.M. on Saturday evening, it was a joyous day around the Carter home. I hadn't spoken to my brother or sister Cynthia prior to that day. My mother and sister told me that morning that they were going shopping and would not be returning home before 6:00 P.M. and if I wanted a ride to the Greyhound bus station I would have to leave with them at that moment. They took me to the bus station about 8:00 A.M., dropped me off and said that they would be back before I left. I sat in that bus station all day by myself, just thinking about this journey that had been so unsuccessful, and trying to build my tenacity. I had not eaten breakfast and did not have the money to buy myself lunch, with dinner fast approaching. It was five forty-five and I remember my bags were already on the bus when my mother and sister walked up to me just before I was about to board, Cynthia, in her enmity, walked up and gave me a five dollar bill. King Solomon wrote in Proverbs 15:19, "The way of the sluggard is blocked with thorns, but the path of the upright is a highway." This was a very awkward moment. They said farewell and asked that I take care of myself. I got on that bus with the intentions of never returning to Richmond again.

The city of Richmond over the years has never been advantageous for me. In fact it proved to be literally stagnate compared to my lifestyle which had become very liberal. But in actuality Richmond is a great city. It's just that as a child growing up there, I can remember telling Malcolm that once I would leave that city. So I assume that each time I left it became easier for me to do so again.

My family did however make it almost impossible for me to stay. In a lot of ways I loved that house on Dabbs House Road that my family lived in, and really could not imagine ever living anywhere else. My father was buried on that property. He had always said that if anything ever happened for us to bury him under a tree on the northeast corner of our property. Unlike my family, I believe this carried a probative sentimental value to me, and I felt that we would live there forever.

Once again I was on the road, however this time I felt sort of like a misfit because I was not ready to return to California. However, before the bus got outside of the Richmond city limits I had forgotten or, at least, I made a conscious effort to put this dreadful situation behind me. Paul wrote to the saints in Philippi, "Brothers, I do not consider myself yet to have taken hold of it. But one thing I do: Forgetting what is behind and straining toward what is ahead" (Philippians 3:13). I was unsure where I would stay when I returned to Seaside. However, I knew that there would be a place for me. That Voice in my head kept telling me that it would be all right. Subconsciously, I set my sights on things ahead. I remember saying a prayer asking God for guidance and wisdom. Also I asked him to provide me a place to stay. Briefly, thoughts of Mandy cluttered my mind. I began to contemplate how my life might have been different if I had gone to Minneapolis with her. I even thought of going there and looking her up, but I did not know where to start. There was one significant difference about this journey across the United States, that being, this time we took the southern route. I had been south before, however only by air, and had never viewed the sights like the bus ride would afford me so I was quite excited.

In Atlanta this very beautiful woman approached me and asked me if I knew Jesus. I said that I did, however I was more interested in her beauty. Jesus Christ said himself in the gospel of Matthew 5:28, "but I tell you that anyone who looks at a woman lustfully has already committed adultery with her in his heart." I asked her about herself and she responded by proclaiming to be a "Georgia Peach." "What is a Georgia Peach?" I asked. And she said, "That is what they call us southern girls down here." Well, we talked a little about God and, considering my recent misfortune, this was one conversation I wanted to avoid. When I finally realized that this Georgia Peach was more interested in my soul and salvation than my body, I abruptly ended our conversation by asking her where was the nearest liquor store. She reluctantly directed me and I was on my way in a hurry because the bus was leaving soon. Unlike my first trip cross-country via bus, there was no Mandy and there was nobody except for myself going clear cross-country. So this trip was rather boring until we reached Texas.

There in Texas the bus was stopped on three separate occasions. Since all of the other black males had gotten off of the bus in Arkansas, each time the troopers stopped the bus in Texas, they pulled me off and ordered me to lie face down while they searched my luggage. The bus driver enlightened me afterwards that this was a common occurrence with African-American males traveling by bus through Texas. He said that they were looking for drug traffickers and he was quite undisturbed by their adverse behavior towards me. Each time that I re-entered the bus the other passengers would stare at me as though I was a convicted serial killer.

I was so happy when the bus crossed the California line. Although I had lived in California for some years, I still felt as if I was starting over again and I welcomed this challenge. In my mind I had become a Californian. There was a yearning for a relationship with my family hidden deep in my soul, but nothing outside of me that reflected Virginia. I had tried that. And I had tried to reconcile with my family. It did not work. If there was ever anything that I was sure of, it was the fact that I was a Californian now, not by choice, but out of necessity. I had come to the conclusion that if I made it in this world I had to forget about Richmond, and so I did.

That night the bus rolled through Los Angeles I remember telling myself that I liked this town. I had been to LA once before one weekend in 1982 when Champ and I had driven there for a weekend of partying and womanizing. However, I hadn't seen LA like I saw it on the Greyhound bus. I had said to myself that one day soon I would return to LA to scout a University, particularly California State University, Los Angeles.

When the bus arrived in Seaside I had mixed feelings. I was happy to be finally over this long journey, but, I felt a little nervous because I did not know where I was going to be staying.

I did not tell anyone that I was returning. Even though it was less than five months since I had left, I knew that my circle of friends had erratic lifestyles, so I did not try to contact them. Instead I went to my ace in the hole, I knew Mel, who was also a Black Panther, would help me even if nobody else would. He invited me to stay in his extra bedroom until I could get myself together. He vowed to help me "by any means necessary" to get back on my feet. This was truly a blessing. Since I had never fulfilled my obligation to the County of Monterey in terms of checking myself into an Alcohol Rehabilitation Program, I began to look into this. I did and settled on SunStreet in Salinas. In early January 1984, I moved into SunStreet.

CHAPTER SIX

SUNSTREET, IGANASIO AND SUCCESS

Salinas is a small industrial town twenty miles southeast of the city of Monterey. Although the residents included farms workers, the population consisted mostly of upper middle class white Americans. Since SunStreet was relatively near Seaside, I could get on the freeway and drive there. Reluctantly, I left Seaside, in my heart knowing that I would never return there to live again. SunStreet was a live-in Alcohol Rehabilitation Center and its inhabitants were comprised of mostly court-ordered participants, but there were also a large contingent of walk-in drug addicts. Ironically, it was located right in the middle of a neighborhood infested with prostitutes and drug dealers. I never have understood how one of the most successful rehabilitation programs, according to the court's standards, could be located in such a deprived neighborhood. However, it was, and the place seemed secluded from the rest of the Salinas community.

I believe that I was committed there at the wrong time in my life. Because had I known then what I know now, I would have used that opportunity to take care of the serious problems that had haunted me most of my life. But I just went there because I needed to fulfill an obligation to the courts. SunStreet was not a free program and one of the requirements was that we apply for welfare and food stamps. We were supposed to turn the food stamps and relief checks over to the staff and they would keep 75% of both, thereby paying for our stay there. The rules stated that our first two weeks at SunStreet we could not leave or have any visitors. Also, we had to participate in kitchen duty. After the two-week period we could seek employment but we had to be in by 10:00 P.M. every night. Since I had never had a job outside of the academic community and needed to make up those additional credits for transferring to the University system, I signed up for classes at Hartnell College. This also provided me with a supplementary income. Hartnell College allowed me the needed time away from SunStreet to drink alcohol and do drugs. However, Hartnell College also afforded me an opportunity to meet Ignasio, who reminded me very much of Robert. He was a Mexican American and the Education Opportunity Program (EOP) Director at that school.

Ignasio seemed to take a legitimate interest in me and, just as Robert had done some years earlier, he appeared to be bent on making me his protégé. This was fine with me because I knew deep inside that God was taking care of me in certain ways. I was still an impressionable young man and believed that these astute, confident young professionals saw something in me that others did not, or refused to acknowledge.

Because of my EOP status I had to have extensive contact with Ignasio. He became my confidant and I valued his opinion in every way—mostly because he seemed to always have it together. So I knew that he would not tell me anything that would prove detrimental. Ignasio was the first person that told me I should leave SunStreet. He knew my situation and urged me to complete the program as soon as possible, then move on. He insisted that I would accomplish more if I had my own apartment. Over the next several months the more he and I interacted, the more self-esteem I developed. And I began to feel confident and assured of my goals. He had this ambiance about him that exuded success. He lead by example and he possessed this "we can do it" attitude. If you did not know him, it could have been mistaken for arrogance. However, this motivated me and I viewed it as confidence.

My EOP counselor was referred to as "Cynthia O," and she was the most erotic person that I had ever met up to that point in my life. She maintained this freedom about herself that was intriguing and laudable. Cynthia O was a very beautiful African-American politically conscious woman, who seemed empowered by her identity. She was very much in touch with reality and I was impressed, to say the least, with her dexterity. She too seemed to take special interest in me. And considering her obscure uniqueness, I took an arousing curiosity in her. The dialogue we engaged in during our association was upbeat and has been reverberant.

Since Cynthia O was my EOP counselor, she had a business stake in my academic progress. Just like Ignasio, she felt I should get out of the SunStreet setting. She always told me that if there was something extraordinary hindering my growth as a spiritual person, I should separate myself from it. Psalms 1:1 tells us, "Blessed is the man who does not walk in the counsel of the wicked or stand in the way of sinners or sit in the seat of mockers." She also was a very spiritual person and introduced me to Buddhism. She told me that by chanting I could become "one with the universe." Although this was interesting there was just something about chanting to a scroll that didn't work for me. Nonetheless, I acknowledged the practice, and after gentle coercion, I attended several meetings with her.

Cynthia O was awaiting notification from San Francisco State University on whether they had hired her for a position. She was the first person to suggest that I seriously start looking into a four-year University. When I was at MPC most of the people who had graduated from there were going either to Fresno State, Chico State or San Jose State. So I immediately eliminated those schools from consideration and began to lean toward a southern California school.

My academic counselor Ms. Green called me into her office one day and asked whether I was aware that I was rapidly approaching the Community College maximum unit level for financial aid. She said that it was getting close to the time for me to transfer. She did not ask me whether I wanted to, just sort of assumed that I did. Since my early days at MPC I had been going to school as a means of support. Suddenly, Ms. Green's comments presented me an opportunity to view my situation from a different perspective. I left her office with a decision to make. She instructed me to let her know what I had decided soon so she could assist me in filing the necessary forms.

Meanwhile I had gotten a work-study position in the disabled students office. Since I had experience in Student Activities, the Director Wayne Davis hired me to coordinate activities for about sixty disabled students at Harnell. This job entailed entire autonomy, which has always brought the best efforts out of me, and this experience proved to be rewarding, partly because this gave me an opportunity to see firsthand another aspect of life. The problem that I thought I had was infinitesimal compared to the daily misfortunes of most of those students.

My co-worker Joanne eventually became my closest confident, next to Iganasio. Fatefully, Joanne represented someone I could talk to at any time because we were spiritually yoked. She was the first Filipino friend I ever had and I welcomed her into my circle. She was a very attractive person who had an innocence about her that superseded every girl I had ever met since Rhonda. Joanne told me all the time that our friendship was too valuable to jeopardize engaging in a romantic fling. We talked a lot about our futures and she was one of the few people that I had confided in about my recent unfavorable experience with my family. She had a very soothing personality and she was, for me, mentally stimulating. She was an extremely intelligent person who seemed to feel a sense of compassion towards me. She had this way about herself that made me feel comfortable around her. I could talk to her when I needed advice, and she went out of her way on many occasions to make herself available whenever I needed to talk. Solomon wrote in Proverbs 12:15, "The way of a fool seems right to him, but a wise man listens to advice." Even though she was younger than me and had not experienced life in ways that I had, she possessed wisdom far beyond that of mine.

VOICES OF MY FATHER

In June of that year, while I was sitting in the office, a young woman walked in and asked in broken English how she could find out more about Hartnell. Since advisement about campus policies and procedures were part of my job, I offered to assist her. Her name was Margarita and she was a beautiful, petite, thick-boned sandy brown El Salvadorian princess. We were attracted to each other and coincidentally had been born on the same day. Her and her two year old daughter had just moved back to Salinas from Germany. She had recently separated from her husband and was looking to start a new life.

As an academic directive, Margarita needed my assistance in helping her get into school. After advising she eventually enrolled in the fall. Subsequently a wonderfully fruitful relationship between us was born. However she was somewhat reserved concerning me because her husband had abandoned her and her daughter unexpectedly and that had an adverse effect on her. Eventually I was able to break through some of those barriers and she began to open up. We went to the beach often and talked. She even went to a SunStreet barbecue with me and understood why I was there. We allowed each other the freedom to express ourselves to one another.

Meanwhile, all those nights of sneaking into SunStreet drunk, after curfew, finally caught up with me. One night I was caught coming in drunk and was given 24 hours to find another place. People used to get thrown out of that place daily and I knew that it was only a matter of time before my indiscretion was exposed. I had already fulfilled my obligation to the county and was rather glad that this happened because it forced me to spread my wings.

Margurita and I trusted each other and she lent me some money to add to some I had saved up in order to rent a room—

so I did, not too far from Hartnell. She lived with her sister, and would come and stay with me from time to time. We initially did not have sex because she was not ready; it was too soon after her previous relationship. This made me respect and love her even more.

In September I informed my counselor that I had narrowed my choices to California State University, Los Angeles or Long Beach campuses. She said that I had made good choices considering that both those schools had excellent business programs, which was my undergraduate major. Cynthia O had been offered that long-awaited job at San Francisco State University and had left Salinas. Joanne had been accepted into San Jose State University and was leaving the next fall so things were rapidly changing.

I was not going to Seaside as much and knew that my time in this area was coming to a close. Although I had applied to CSULB, I finally decided on CSULA because of the financial aid package they offered. The California State Department of Rehabilitation agreed to help facilitate the transition process because of my past commitment at SunStreet, which helped out tremendously.

January 1985 came and I still had not received an answer from either school. One day, while I was talking outside of the Disabled Students office, Joanne approached me and said that my mother was on the phone. Initially, I thought she was joking, however Joanne did not joke like that. Yet I also knew that my family did not know where I was. Joanne said that she was not joking and insisted that I come to the phone. I told her that if it was my mother, tell her that I did not want to speak to her. Joanne said that she was not going to tell her that and persuaded me to come to the phone. Reluctantly I picked up the phone and sure enough it was my mother's voice. She said to me that they had not heard from me in over a year and felt she should try to contact me. Apparently, she had called the Student Activities Office at MPC and spoke with Bonnie, who informed her of my whereabouts. We briefly spoke somberly—a conversation that was filled with resentment and melancholy. I told her that I was awaiting an acceptance letter from those schools. She said that she just wanted to know whether I was still alive. Since there was no place for her to contact me, she asked me to keep in touch and we bid each other farewell. Deep inside my soul I was glad to hear from her although I was in perpetual pain, scarred for life. After I hung that phone up I remember that Voice again telling me things would be different.

About the end of January, I still had not heard anything from those schools and was beginning to experience periods of anxiety. I paid Ms. Green a visit to voice my concern and she concurred and agreed to call the schools for me. She informed me that I had indeed been accepted into my first choice, CSULA, but the letter had yet to arrive. Suddenly I knew that things would definitely be different and the conversion project began. Ms. Green told me that I had been accepted into the Spring Quarter, which would be beginning in mid-March. This gave me about a month to prepare. The EOP office instructed her that I needed to come to Los Angeles for a day, as soon as possible, to find housing and enroll in my classes. So that Monday I left about 2:30 A.M. for Los Angeles.

I was extremely excited about this transition, although I did not really know anyone except my buddy 'June' in LA. Yet I welcomed this challenge because it represented a new beginning.

I was only going to be in Los Angeles for a day so I knew that I had better take care of business. When I arrived on campus I told the attendant at the Kiosk that I was an EOP transfer student and knew nothing about the University. He asked me my name, then called the EOP office and informed them that I was downstairs. The EOP office sent a student worker down with a parking pass and we went up to the office.

Upon arriving at the EOP office I was introduced to Becky, who ultimately proved very important in my development as a serious student. She already had my file and she knew that I had been in an Alcohol Rehabilitation Center because that was the address that was listed on all my records. She asked me many questions, some personal, some not so personal. I told her that I would only be in LA for a day. She said that we had a lot to do in a relatively short period of time so we got right to business. Becky also informed me that the University had just opened a housing facility and asked if I wanted to move there. Since I did not have a place to stay or even a lead, I said sure. She told me after we take care of our initial business she would direct me to the Housing Office. When I was a little kid I always wanted to experience living in the dorm. The closest I had come to even seeing a dormitory was when I had taken Rhonda to Fresno State.

Becky and I sat in her office and talked most of the day. She said that she wanted to get me out of there before 3:00 P.M. because the traffic would be extremely congested after that. She put together a program and stipulated that if I followed it and passed all of my classes I would graduate in about a year and a half. Or, I could choose to take it slow and still graduate with a Bachelors degree in about two years. Becky was an alumni of CSULA and was extremely knowledgeable about the University.

She seemed to know everything and was an attractive, personable woman who earned my trust right away. I believed her, and something Divine inside of me made me draw closer to her. The prophet Isaiah wrote, "Whether you turn to the right or to the left, your ears will hear a voice behind you, saying, 'This is the way; walk in it' (Isaiah 30.221). After we finished our business she asked one of the students to show me the campus and housing office. After that she said we would visit the financial aid office where my paperwork had already been completed. The campus was spacious and beautiful. I knew finally that I had made it to the big time and was confident that I would not only fit in but excel. I was determined to prove to myself that I could succeed. There were not too many people on campus because of the break, and this proved to be beneficial because it afforded me an opportunity to get the special attention I so much needed. The University had everything it was supposed to have. The library was huge with a roof where I could retreat, pray, and meditate.

Time was moving rather fast and I knew that I could not enjoy myself too much because this was not that kind of trip. There were many other important issues left to be taken care of and Becky was waiting. In Housing I was told there was definitely a place that could be reserved for me. The Director was more interested in my financial aid status than in me, which was normal because I knew that he was just doing his job. I explained that I was an EOP student and would be receiving full financial aid and assistance from the Department of Rehabilitation. He really became interested in me at that point—I assume because the housing costs would come directly out of my financial aid.

Next I was shown an apartment which looked more like a condominium. Each apartment had two bedrooms with two beds in each bedroom. He told me that he was unsure which apartment I would be in, but he assured me that a spot would be reserved and asked me when I would be moving in. I told him that I was still living in Salinas and would be moving to LA sometime in early March. He than gave me a questionnaire and stated that this was a formality, intended to assist the staff with matching roommates for me.

Becky and I then went to the financial aid office. She had taken the liberty to make an appointment for us to sit down with Kim, my financial aid counselor. Kim was an extremely serious person. She talked like a robot and her demeanor signified business. At that moment I became aware that she was probably the most important person in this journey. She informed me that it would not be financially difficult for me to complete my degree if I focused on my objective. They were unaware, that I did not know then what that objective was. Kim told me that that unfortunate stay in SunStreet was actually fortunate in terms of financial aid. She informed me that between the department of rehabilitation and the University that I would have my entire tuition and books paid for—and went on to say that they had put together a rather generous financial aid package. Also she informed me that my housing costs would come directly out of my Pell Grant. She told me that I was eligible for a loan or work-study. Ever since I had started college at MPC I had been a recipient of work-study and was very familiar with this program. She said that she did not know where there was a position open, but Becky interceded at that point to say that there was someone she thought might be interested in hiring me. Kim took all the forms that Becky had prepared and suddenly I was enrolled as a junior at California State University, Los Angeles. I thanked Kim and assured her that our relationship would be fruitful and enlightening for both of us.

Becky reminded me that it was approaching 3:00 P.M. She suggested since I had been working in Student Activities I could possibly get a job as a Peer Advisor in the Advisement and Counseling Center. She took me there and introduced me to Bill who seemed to be glad to meet me. Once he heard that I was enrolled and had full financial aid with experience in Student Advisement, he hired me on the spot. Bill told us that when I arrived back in LA and got settled in to come to start work.

Becky and I went to her office for some final instructions. She told me this had been one of her more productive days as a counselor, as indeed it was for me as a person. In one day I had enrolled in the University system, gotten housing, a liberal financial package and a job. I had met people and established a network. There had never been one single day in my life that I had accomplished so much in a seven hour period. The Lord told us in Isaiah 45:2, "I will go before you and will level the mountains, I will break down gates of bronze and cut through bars of iron." There before me was my future, waiting. I sincerely thanked Becky and asked her how could I ever repay her for all that she had done for me. She said I could thank her by succeeding and just finishing what I was about to start, I assured her that I would. She told me to contact her when I got back in Los Angeles. We said our good-byes and I left for Salinas.

All I could think about on my journey back was how I was being blessed. I knew how excited I was for myself. But there was something else that continued to press on my mind, those Voices of my Father. I thought of Margarita also. She had been the closest person to me over the last several months and I knew that she had just started Hartnell; however a part of me wanted to bring her with me.

An awful yet predictable occurrence happened on the trip back when I was stopped by a Highway Patrol for what they said was "suspicious behavior." They informed me that they were looking for young African-American males traveling alone from LA that could possibly be transferring drugs. This was the furthest thing from my mind, but all of a sudden I started thinking about drugs and how I was going to celebrate when I got back to Salinas.

The officers asked for my license so I showed it to them. It was apparent I was not impaired and, in my opinion, they were exhibiting extremely obtuse behavior. They asked me where I was going and where I was coming from. I told them that I was going home. They asked where was home, I told them. They said that I was a long ways from there. When they asked where I was coming from and I said LA, they asked me if I would object to them searching my car. Since I knew I really had no choice I agreed. However, I also knew what they were capable of and never took my eyes off of them.

After an intense search of my vehicle they appeared agitated—apparently because they did not find any drugs or weapons. They asked why I had been in Los Angeles. I told them that I had been down there registering for college. They answered with belligerent cynicism and sarcasm and told me they would be following me for a while and warned that I had better watch myself because they surely would be watching my every move. The Lord said to Ezekiel, "son of man, these are the men who are plotting evil and giving wicked advice in the city" (Ezekiel 11:2). Police have been harassing young African-American males since the beginning of time. I had been harassed many times in my life for just doing what the United States

Constitution said I could. And it has always bothered me profoundly and could have contributed to the many reasons I left the Commonwealth of Virginia. However, this time, because of the success and progress I had experienced at CSULA, this harassment, in its own pathetic way, only slowed my travel.

CHAPTER SEVEN

COMPOSURE FOR THE 10TH

I wanted somehow to convince Margarita to come with me to Los Angeles. But I also knew deep inside this was something I needed to do by myself. I still could not shake this feeling as I was driving back to Salinas that I would be leaving behind someone who had become so important to me. It was during that drive back I realized my true feelings for her. Somehow I would have to resolve those feelings. My late arrival back in Salinas prevented me from calling her about my good news. This provided me with an additional night to collect my thoughts. I knew there was a lot of business that I had to take care of quickly and I needed to put together a plan of action.

The next day I went to Hartnell and withdrew from all of my classes. Hartnell was a semester system college, currently in the midst of a term. I had a conversation with Ignasio and told him about my good fortune. He was extremely supportive of my decision and wrote me a letter of recommendation. He advised me of what I was about to embark upon which was helpful. He told me how the quarter system moved faster than the semester system. I went to the Disabled Students office and spoke to Wayne, who was also supportive and agreed to write a letter of recommendation. He too agreed that this would prove favorable for me.

Joanne, my trusted confidant, had mixed feelings. Since she had first committed to San Jose State University I sensed she was anticipating that I would go north with her. She was completing her A.A. degree and would not be transferring until the fall. We sat and talked and although I had never known Joanne to drink alcohol, she suggested we go to the park before I left and toast on a bottle of champagne, which we did.

I was really not looking for Margarita and I did not have to. She knew my schedule and found me as I was completing my conversation with Joanne, who was aware of my relationship with Margarita and politely excused herself. Margarita immediately asked how it had gone in Los Angeles. I informed her that God had His hand on me and that it went extremely well. I told her that I had set a timetable and would be leaving Salinas on the 10th of March forever. Although I could see that she was happy about this progression I felt a presence of abdication. She was disappointed that I would be leaving her. Acts14:22 says, strengthening the disciples and encouraging them to remain true to the faith. " We must go through many hardships to enter the kingdom of God, they said." She had grown accustomed to me being there for her. And although she was a year older I felt as though she had formed a certain dependence on me. This was an extremely awkward moment that I will never forget.

I left the campus of Hartnell College for the last time. I went to discuss my plans with my landlord and he was accommodating—even agreeing to release me from my contractual obligations and affording me unlimited time to move out. TJ, my friend who lived alone not far from me, allowed me to stay with him until I left. He was an Army Sergeant stationed at Fort Ord in Monterey. TJ was also a heroin addict. I had known many addicts in my life. However with the exception of my time at SunStreet I did not really have much contact with them. But TJ was my friend and I was deeply concerned about his problem, primarily because once while I was visiting a friend in Seaside a solider stopped over and requested to use his restroom. He allowed him and an hour later we noticed that he had not come out. So we went to the door and called his name and he did not answer, we knew something was wrong. I opened the door to find his stiff leg lodged against it and he was sprawled on the bathroom floor with a syringe in his arm. I checked for a pulse but there was none. He was dead, apparently he wanted to use the restroom to "slam" heroin. The police later said that there was a bad drug going around called "China White." I will never forget the look on that soldier's face, his paleness and that stillness.

That wicked experience provoked my special interest in TJ. Although I was familiar with drug use and drug users, heroin is a drug I never wanted to try. I guess because I had seen firsthand what it could do. And although I would not admit it, subconsciously I was afraid of it. I do not believe that Voice I had grown accustomed to hearing would have allowed me to try this fatal drug anyway. Every heroin addict that I have ever known had this bad karma about themselves. In fact every drug addict seemed to be possessed by an evil spirit. TJ was different. I liked him and was determined to help him kick this habit, and the foundation of our friendship was centered around my intentions. Since I would be leaving soon I intensified my efforts. I did not want my good friend to end up like that soldier. And I could not delegate this responsibility to a mutual friend Gerald because he was a crack addict. His addiction, in my opinion, was just as severe as TJ's, however Gerald could not function.

I assumed in many ways my departure would be bittersweet. Bitter, because I was leaving my friends in a state of disarray, and sweet, because I was beginning a new life, getting a second chance. The Department of Rehabilitation promised to help facilitate my move to Los Angeles. They agreed to pay for the gasoline, to have my car serviced and also to pay my tuition and buy some clothing for my trip. They agreed to continue to pay my tuition as long as I was maintaining a "C" average. They told me that the day before I left, to come and pick up a check for $1,000. They informed me that I should go to the Social Services Department to get some food stamps to help me once I got to Los Angeles and I did. Suddenly I realized that I had taken care of all of my business and just had to wait for the 10th of March to arrive.

Cynthia O introduced me to an attorney friend of hers named Phyllis. She was a forceful person—meaning that she would do almost anything to get her point across. Phyllis was also Buddhist and wanted very much to convert me to Buddhism. When she heard that I was moving to Los Angeles she made a point to spend as much time with me as possible. I had attested in the past I was a Christian for life. I could not see how chanting to a scroll could change my life. So I rejected Phyllis' claims, just as I had Cynthia O's, and both TJ and I became very annoyed by her persistence. I remember TJ once becoming very agitated by her actions and requested that she leave his home.

As the 10th of March approached anxiety began to overcome me, much like that of a kid anticipating Santa's arrival, realizing this was not just another trip to Santa Cruz or Oakland. I was really about to relocate to Los Angeles—feelings of confusion, uncertainty and fear of the unknown began to encompass me.

Finally March 9th approached and Margarita and I spent that entire day together. We went to the beaches in Monterey, also affording me a last opportunity to say good-bye to my friends in Seaside. She and I spent a passionate night together expressing ourselves unlike we had ever done previously. Deep inside both of our hearts we knew that these final moments together represented the end of something special. However we agreed that one day in the future we would again meet up and express our love in a more mature fashion. Margarita asked me to call her often and we kissed and parted forever.

March 10th arrived and because I wanted to be on the freeway while no one else was, I left at 3:00 A.M. I loaded the car with the last of my personal items and set out for Los Angeles. As I was leaving the county of Monterey I could not help but think of everything that I had been through over the years in Seaside and Salinas. There was that Voice again; however unlike the previous times that Voice appeared I was unsure that this was my earthly father's voice. Suddenly I knew that there was definitely a destiny that was pulling me toward Los Angeles.

During that five-hour drive through dense fog, many thoughts came to my mind. However there were no thoughts that were stronger than the thought of Margarita. I hadn't been close to a person like her in my entire life and felt that I might have been letting her down somewhat—after all we had become best friends.

I arrived in Los Angeles about 9:00 A.M. and went directly to CSULA. Upon my arrival at the housing facility I noticed that the campus was extremely empty. Most of the students had left campus and were enjoying spring break. I welcomed this because I am someone who likes to be familiar with his surroundings. All this was extremely new to me and gave me an opportunity to scout my new environment.

Upon my arrival at CSULA the housing attendant said that I would be sharing an apartment with three athletes—one basketball player and two baseball players. She went on to say that they were all gone, probably until the Spring Quarter started, which meant I would have the apartment to myself for a while.

The housing facility was located down an enormous amount of stairs and in order to get to the main campus we had to walk up those stairs. So after getting settled in I walked up to the main campus. On the way to Becky's office I remember seeing a gentleman sitting under a tree. He appeared to be a vagabond and he was wearing old clothes and had a ragged beard. He also was reading a Bible and noticed I was staring at him. He acknowledged me by saying "righteous." I answered him by saying hello. I remember that he had this table set up with a jar full of quarters and was burning incense.

When I arrived in Becky's office I told her about what I had seen. She told me that was "Sunshine' and he was the campus mascot, so to speak. She then enlightened me that Sunshine has been a permanent fixture on the campus for years. She suggested that I sit and exchange dialogue with him when the time permitted. Becky and I went over my program and schedule once again. We finalized all the necessary paperwork for financial aid and I was officially a student at CSULA. This was a very satisfying feeling, especially because ever since I was a little boy I had always been fascinated by the idea of being a University student. Even though I hadn't taken or set foot in a class as yet, this represented a moment in my life when I felt a sense of accomplishment. I realized in a brief instant that I had made it to the big time, but I could not help but remember all those days when my friends and I wasted time at the beach in Monterey discussing what Universities we would be attending.

After Becky and I finished our business she made an appointment for me to come in and see her in about two weeks. Classes were starting in about a week and she wanted to talk with me after that, so if there were any classes that proved too tough for me we could adjust them. I agreed and rightfully so because CSULA operates on the Quarter system, contrary to the Semester system that I was accustomed to.

I went to visit Bill in the Student Advisement and Counseling Center after leaving EOP. He introduced me to his secretary Dorothy, who was notably reading the Bible. At once Sunshine came to mind and I subsequently made up my mind to go speak with him. Bill was a very large man with a Ph.D in Psychology. He seemed to be a fair man. However, unlike with my mentors in Junior College, I do not think I ever allowed myself to become attached to him in certain ways, although he was extremely wise and served as the University Ombudsman. He appointed me as head of the counter which meant I had to become very knowledgeable about campus policies and procedures rather quickly. I received this responsibility with gratitude and sincerity and this gave me an opportunity to learn the ins and outs about the University. We agreed that I should take the rest of the day to familiarize myself with the campus.

During my tenure in Junior college I had always been a part of Student Government in some capacity, so I visited the Student Union to check out the Student Government facilities. There on that day I must have met about 100 students or more. When I walked in the Office of Student Government on the fourth floor I met two clerks. One was an Hispanic-American male named Fred who was in his early forties, the other was named Yolanda, an African-American in her early thirties. Both were extremely knowledgeable about the University. Fred's history with the University went all the way back to the 60s. Yolanda's tenure with the University went back to the early 80s.

I was unaware then but those two individuals would become very close friends of mine for years to come. They told me everything about CSULA from registration procedures to the upcoming student elections. Fred and I agreed to meet later at the Pub, an on-campus watering hole where they served beer and wine. Yolanda and I talked longer and eventually she introduced me to Robert, the student body president. He was an extremely busy person; however once he heard that I was a seasoned student politician he quickly instructed his secretary to make an appointment for us to meet at length. He thanked Yolanda for introducing us and for some reason I got the impression there was an award that went along with this introduction and found out later that indeed it was. Robert needed some additional politically proactive students to help his administration with their agenda. Although he was a "white boy" we quickly formed an alliance.

Yolanda and I went and got something to eat. We talked for hours and she became my first friend in Los Angeles. She told me how her family had treated her in the past. She also mentioned how she and her oldest sister had a "falling out." She told me how her mother and other siblings had just kicked her out of the family. This brought us closer together because I had gone through similar experiences with my family. Solomon wrote, "If one falls down, his friend can help him up. But pity the man who falls and has no one to help him up" (Ecclesiastes 4:10). We developed a bond that has lasted ever since.

Although Yolanda was working toward a master's in education at CSULA, she was temporarily living on campus at the University of Southern California. She asked me to take her home, so she could show me some of the sights in Los Angeles, which was just what I needed. So I took Yolanda back to the USC campus. Since I would be making the return trip to CSULA campus alone, I paid close attention to where we were going. Once we arrived at Yolanda's building I remember thanking her as she was exiting my car. When she invited me up to her room I began to question her motives. Sensing my apprehension she assured me that I could trust her.

While sitting in Yolanda's room we began to talk about God. I explained to her that I had been brought up in a devoutly Christian household and had a good comprehension of the Bible. She invited me to go to church with her in the near future and

I accepted. She then invited me to have dinner with her but I declined because it was getting late and I knew that I had to drive back to CSULA. I thanked her again for everything that she had done for me. We agreed that each of us had found a new friend and we would be spending some more time together.

During my ride back to CSULA I could not avoid reflecting on my past day, which was profoundly unlike any of my days in Monterey. It had progressed at an extremely fast pace and even though it was my first in Los Angeles, three people had spoken with me about God. I didn't know why, although there was that Voice again telling me that something significant was about to happen.

A few days later as classes started more and more people began to move into the dorms. I knew who my roommates were but I hadn't met them yet. One day I came back into the apartment and there Chris was sitting. He was the star pitcher on the baseball team and had been assigned to the other bedroom, his roommate was Arl, who stood seven feet tall and was on the basketball team. My roommate Jimmy was also a member of the baseball team, but from what I had heard he was not a star and was struggling just to stay on the team. Chris and I got along well and he informed me that neither Arl nor Jimmy would be back until just before classes started. He told me that Arl was hardly ever home and Jimmy spent a significant amount of time over at his girlfriend's house.

Classes started at the end of March and I was experiencing anxiety, for I knew that I would be meeting many new people. My first class was a Pan-African Composers course which fulfilled an Arts requirement and was culturally centered. Since this was primarily an Ethnic Studies course, the students enrolled in the class were almost entirely African-American. Jackie was the instructor and was very much a disciplinarian. She informed us from the beginning that just because this was an Ethnic Studies course we should not view it as an easy grade and I soon found out that she was right. Jackie was a wonderfully gifted singer and was learned in the African-American renaissance era. The apostle Paul wrote to Timothy, "Do not neglect your gift, which was given you through a prophetic message when the body of elders laid hands on you" (1 Timothy 4:14). She instructed us on every African-American composer from Betsy Smith to Quincy Jones.

This class provided me with a cultural experience that has superseded any other in my life. Jackie was also a counselor in the EOP office; she taught me that it was indeed a fulfilling experience to study. She was aware this was my first class in the University system and did not let up on me. Actually she was extremely tough on me and seemed to demand more of me than she did of the other students. She inquisitively approved my research project which was on Paul Robeson. I chose him because of his diversity and knew there would be a lot of information on him to discern. In picking Paul Robson, I pretty much assured myself of a decent grade.

There was a young graduate student in that class named Lareese. She was a beautiful girl, very personable and knew exactly what it meant to be a friend. She told me that she took interest in me because of my straightforward personality. She said I spoke up in class on all issues and seemed to have strong views, personally and politically. She inquired whether I had visited Student Government, citing that I would make a vital student representative. I informed her that I had met Robert and we would be sitting down in the near future discussing a possible role for me within his administration. She said that was fine but suggested that at some point in the future I might want my own administration. I asked Lareese out for a date but she declined, stating that it would be better for us to remain friends because of our politically conscious minds. Proverbs 27:17 tells us, "As iron sharpens iron, so one man sharpens another." I respected and understood exactly what she was advocating.

Meanwhile I had been spending a lot of time with Fred and Yolanda. Fred was working for both the Testing Center and Student Government. I asked him on several occasions why he worked so much, being a student, and he told me that he was living with his mother who was a very old lady. He informed me that she was unable to pay all of her bills and that he helped her out a lot. After Fred told me that—I'm not sure if he ever knew this—but I felt his admirable deeds were commendable and I began to view him in a different light. We would meet in the Pub and have drinks. He became almost immediately one of my best friends and seemed to understand me in a lot of ways that others did not. Fred introduced me to his supervisor Richard who took a liking to me and told me that if I ever wanted to come to work for him in the Testing Center I could.

One night I finally met Arl and Jimmy. We all sat down and had a meeting, laying out the ground rules, which went well. I did not know how they would react to me being the only black and non-athlete. But they received me very favorably and I believed in Arl's case the fact that he was on the basketball team afforded him opportunity to be familiar with African-American culture. As for Jimmy and Chris, they seemed indifferent, apparently they just wanted a compatible roommate and I was determined to give them one. We all got along almost like brothers.

Arl even invited me to his family's home in Monrovia. His family were down-to-earth people and they were not in the least bit uncomfortable about our relationship. I found out later that Arl's mother's boyfriend was African-American. Essentially Arl had been raised around people of color. This explained why we had developed, in a short period of time, the fruitful relationship we had. Because of Arl's popularity a lot of people frequented our apartment. This presented an opportunity for me to meet other students, especially the " in crowd." Since most of them were not yet twenty-one years of age, I would buy alcohol for all of us—at their expense. Before I knew it our apartment had become the "party dorm." There were girls, drugs and alcohol, all three in excess abundance. Classes became secondary in almost no time at all. We would go to class drunk, high and hung over.

There was a bright spot in all this turmoil, there were Olympic athletes around. The Women's Track Team consisted of several world class sprinters who had won Gold Medals in the 1984 Los Angeles Olympic Games. These gifted women knew what success was all about and they had tasted victory at the highest level. Their stalwart success had always intrigued me and quite frankly had a contagious effect on everyone associated with them. They would always pull me off to the side and make comments such as, "you do not seem to be like the rest of them." They would tell me that it seemed as if I was denying myself my destiny by indulging in all that alcohol and drugs. Deep inside I knew they were right because I wanted to change my ways. However there was something that they were not right about, and that was, I was "one of them" and in many ways I had become conspicuously the center of everything that was going on in the dorms during those years.

Several of those women took an interest in me. However

only one became my friend. Deanna was her name and I was fascinated by her because she would always go off by herself during the parties. She told me one evening that she was "into God" and she did not feel comfortable with all this partying. She urged me to leave my ways behind and press forward toward my goal. "Then those who feared the Lord talked with each other, and the Lord listened and heard. A scroll of remembrance was written in his presence concerning those who feared the Lord and honored his name" (Malachi 3:16). I did not understand why she took an interest in me. However, she, just like, Lareese and Yolanda, just wanted to be my friend.

Almost immediately for several reasons I had become very well known on campus in a short period of time, both because of the excessive partying that took place in my apartment, and because of my employment in Advisement and Counseling which provided me first contact with new students. Although I was also a new student you would not have known it because of my knowledge of the campus. I was living two lives and those few who had become part of my inner circle knew of my indiscretions, but fortunately the people who mattered the most did not.

CHAPTER EIGHT

EMBANKMENT

After only being on campus for a couple of months during my meeting with Robert, the newly elected student body president, he appointed me as CSULA representative to the Los Angeles Collegiate Council Board. This appointment yielded the occasion to once again become acquainted with some of the student leaders I had known from my Junior college days—particularly Steve who was now a representative of UCLA. He and I had started a Community College Student Association while he was at San Jose City College and I was at MPC. Steve was an effective, scrupulous motivator and seemed to always take the correct position whenever important issues were on the table. He possessed this 1960s radicalism and most of what I had become as a student leader I owed to him. We came from the same side of the political spectrum and we were sincere about the 1980s student agenda.

In those days a lot of the student leaders in the University system had hidden agendas. A lot of them seemed to be jockeying for positions in public service and we attended many conferences then. The most politically conscious students I had ever met seemed to come out of UCLA. I assume this was the case because that University offered an MBA/LAW degree program where you can earn both degrees simultaneously. I met literally hundreds of students from all over the world enrolled in that program. And I seemed to acquire knowledge from each of them as we shared our experiences. They were extremely aggressive and meticulous in diplomacy. They seemed to take each issue individually in a personal, yet very collective professional manner. They were under continual scrutiny and undoubtedly set the standard in California student politics.

This opportunity allowed me to converse with people who seemed as determined as I was to make a difference in this world. Also those students seemed to come from a social class higher than any to which I had been accustomed. They were extremely articulate and made me realize that although I was rather learned and cultured at that point in my life, there was still room for refinement. Several of the African-American males asked me to consider transferring to UCLA. After meeting and talking with them I was seriously considering it. However I knew there were many important relationships on the CSULA campus that would not have been easy to walk away from. Notwithstanding I appreciated the offer; they gave me a goal to labor for.

Meanwhile back on the CSULA campus I had met by chance a gentleman named Kev. He and I became close and developed an association that went a long way. He was a past member of the basketball team and a native of St. Croix, Virgin Islands. He was about 6 feet 5 inches tall and weighted about 240 pounds. He spoke with a strong Caribbean accent and worked in the Veterans Affairs office. He knew, just as I did, the ins and the outs of the federal financial aid program. He too was an independent student living in the dorms. Since I had not seen him at any of the parties I asked him why. He replied that he had his own sort of parties and invited me to one. I accepted his invitation and one afternoon I went to Kev's dorm. Upon my arrival I met a close friend of his named Mike. He was from Washington, D.C. and since I was from Richmond we had, at least, that in common.

We all became very close friends and did many things together. We were all alike in the sense that we were independent and a long ways from our native homes. We took our already obstinate drug habits to another level since we were all bona fide money makers and spent literally thousands of dollars on crack cocaine. I had tried crack in the late 1970s and early 80s occasionally in Monterey. However the first time that I took it in Southern California was truly a memorable experience. One day we bought a half gram which cost us about fifty dollars—Kev and Mike hit it first. I had always experimented with different drugs in my life and have never really been scared of them; however for some odd reason I was apprehensive about trying this crack—probably because I had not used any since my days in Seaside. But still, I reluctantly smoked a small piece and the feeling was nothing like that I was used to. I immediately felt this overwhelming dizziness and had to sit down and regain my composure. I remember Kev and Mike asking me had I ever done that before. I assured them that I had and it's just we used to "rock" our own.

In the mid-eighties in Monterey you could not buy cocaine in rock form. If you wanted to smoke it you would have to buy the powder and cook the cocaine yourself. This represented the first time that I was smoking something that was presented as crack cocaine. Yet I really did not know what it was. But I knew what it was supposed to be, which was probably the main reason I was a little skeptical about trying it in the first place. 1 Samuel 8:3 tells us, "But his sons did not walk in his ways. They turned aside after dishonest gain and accepted bribes and perverted justice." There were many nights and days we got together and got high.

Because of my escalated drug use I no longer spent much time with my basketball buddies, who basically were doing the same things I was doing but at a much different level. Yolanda started to notice something different about me. However she just could not put her finger on it. She asked why I was no longer spending much time on campus or around her. She was persistent in her efforts to get me to go to church with her. Subconsciously, I was avoiding her because I knew that I was living in the fast lane once again. The disciple Luke wrote, "As they talked and discussed these things with each other, Jesus himself came up and walked along with them; but they were kept from recognizing him" (Luke 24:15). I did not like that guilty feeling she was unknowingly making me have.

At work one day in late spring of 1985 I called my mother because I had not spoken with her since that day at Hartnell. She did not know where I was so I needed to let her know. All those counseling sessions with my beloved friend Yolanda had begun to pay dividends. When my mother found out where I was she seemed blissful. My mother is a very arduous individual to figure out—one can never predict how she will react. However I have always admired her candor in her interactions with me. We talked a little about my transition and she seemed genuinely happy to hear that I was now in the University system. I told her my address and she agreed to write me from time to time.

The Advisement and Counseling Center provided me refuge in more ways than one. Dorothy seemed to automatically take the same role as Bonnie had during my years at MPC. However, unlike Bonnie, Dorothy studied her Bible all day. She would read that Bible for literally hours. We talked in detail about the Scriptures and she seemed surprised to find out that I knew as much as I did about the Bible and salvation. I informed her that I had been reared by devout Christian parents. I told her about my life and about some of the vices that had hindered my Christian growth over the years. I told her about my estrangement from my family. She seemed to understand why I was somewhat of an introvert. Over the years I have always maintained a longing in my heart for a substantial relationship with my family. She said she had had similar experiences growing up.

After that conversation Dorothy and I seemed to have established a new relationship. She became more protective of me and would advise me in a sisterly tone that I could respect. Subtly she continued to ask that I accompany her to church. "Therefore, dear friends, since you already know this, be on your guard so that you may not be carried away by the error of lawless men and fall from your secure position" (2 Peter 3:17). I never went with her; however I sincerely believe that had it not been for those real moments we shared together I might have been lost to the Kingdom forever.

During one of those weekly visits to Becky's office she told me that she was pregnant and would be leaving once she had progressed to her eighth month. She said that there would be someone else taking over her case load. I had developed somewhat of a dependency on her. And I considered her partly responsible for my transition into the student I had become. I felt extremely comfortable with her, and since I was not a trusting person, I became very concerned about what was transpiring. Becky assured me that she would one day return and that she would not be leaving until the Summer Quarter. We mapped out a plan that would take me clear to graduation.

I had not visited June since I had been in Los Angeles. He had told me several times that he had four sisters and a brother. He also suggested that I look him up when I moved to Los Angeles. I had told him that I would but up until that point I really did not want to leave the campus.

Yolanda had shown me around Los Angeles. So one day I called the number June had given me and his mother answered and introduced herself as Mae. She was a nice-sounding woman and promptly invited me over, so I went and met her entire family. I met Jana, Jimmy, Stanky, Renee, Joe Lee, Booty, Chris, Jalon and Bay Boy—all of them were extremely beautiful, nice and fun to be around people. They were a close family and possessed Southern Baptist ties. I was immediately welcomed into their family almost like a surrogate brother. June had told me that it would be this way.

Back on campus finals were rapidly approaching and, in my

opinion, too quickly. I had been attending my classes regularly and was prepared for my first finals. Becky had assigned me to some pretty easy classes so that I would do well. And, as expected, I did. Finally classes were over. Everyone was going their separate ways. I was unsure of my living situation but the housing director assured me everyone who wanted to stay for the summer could. All of my roommates were moving out, contesting that it was too expensive to live there. The Summer Quarter was a bit boring but it gave me an opportunity to concentrate on my studies in depth. I had attended the convocation the week prior and had visions of one day graduating myself.

    A catastrophic life-changing event happened at the beginning of summer. I was invited over to June's house to see an NBA Final's game between the Los Angeles Lakers and the Boston Celtics. On my way to his home I stopped and picked up some alcohol. Although three of his sisters and his brother Joe were at this party, it seemed as if June and I were the only two who got drunk. After the Lakers lost I attempted to drive home. His family pleaded with me to sleep there but I declined.

    Within a few minutes I was heading east on the Santa Monica freeway when I almost immediately lost control of the wheel. My car flipped, it seemed five or six times, before I landed in the embankment along the side of the road. I struggled out of the car and began to stagger in the middle of the freeway. Cars were swerving to miss me, traveling in excess of eighty miles an hour. I was in the middle of the freeway walking when an LAPD patrol car stopped along the side of the embankment. An officer ran out where I was staggering in the middle of the freeway and pulled me by the arm to the side of his car. They had passed my car in the embankment. And it did not take a rocket scientist to see that I was drunk. They arrested me for drunk driving and took me to Parker Center, or "The Glasshouse" as it is more commonly known.

I must have been very uncooperative and they became extremely forceful with me. My thought and perception were somewhat blurred during this time. However I would soon receive a rude awakening. I remember one of the officers telling me to shut up. I then remember this strong electrical current going through my body. I lost all control of my limbs and bodily functions. I defecated on myself and fell to the floor. I remember a officer shouting at me to get up. The last thing I remember was another electrical current rushing through my body. My next state of consciousness was when I awoke to the sound of a tin cup brushing back and forth across the bars of a cell where I was housed. Although this cell had fifty or more bunks in it I was the only occupant. I remember looking to the front of the cell to see an inmate standing outside the bars with a cup.

He asked whether I was all right. I said, although I had dried defecation on me, that I seemed fine. All of a sudden I noticed this burning feeling on my back. Suddenly it all started to come back to me. The inmate trustee told me that I had been there for a couple of days by myself. I asked him where I was. He said that I was in the "Glasshouse" and the jail attendants ordered him to come back there periodically to check on me. He said this was the first time I had responded to his "rattling of the cage." He said that he personally thought I was dead. And those burning sensations I was feeling in my back probably were the result of a weapon with two electrical prongs called a Taser.

This was the first time that I had come into contact with the infamous LAPD. I had heard and read a lot about these policemen and what they were capable of. Quite frankly, I had made a pact with myself that I was going to avoid them as much as I could. But considering my present predicament this had quickly become another broken promise. I had also heard about the Taser. It was widely reported they were experimenting with this new crime-fighting apparatus and I suspect that I was a subject of experimentation. Unfortunately I almost lost my life and believed that I was put in that large cell because just in case I died they could blame it on the other inmates. The irony to all of this is they had probably saved my life on that freeway a couple of nights earlier.

I asked the trustee to inform the police that I had regained consciousness—so he did. A jail attendant came to get me. They informed me that I was being charged with drunk driving. And they told me that I would be booked and cited out. They said that they would be notifying me by mail of a court date. I emphatically asked the location of my car. They said it was impounded and that I would have to contact them to see what was necessary for me to get it back. So that morning, two days after my accident, I was released from the "Glasshouse" in downtown Los Angeles.

Sitting at the bus stop I could not avoid thinking of Monterey. Several times I had escaped death in almost the same manner. Less than a year earlier, while driving a new car I had bought, while at SunStreet, I ran head on into a telephone pole at high speed. On that occasion I got out of the car unhurt and was walking along the freeway. Someone picked me up that night and took me to my front door. Psalms 91:4 explicitly assures us, "He will cover you with his feathers, and under his wings you will find refuge; his faithfulness will be your shield and rampart."

To this very day I do not know who that someone was, where that person came from, or even if that person knew me. All I knew was I had come face to face with death, only to be saved by the grace of God. I thought of that New Year's Eve night when Big James and I were en route to Rhonda's. While I was sitting at that bus stop I thought about many of my blessings. I did not tell any of my peers what had happened to me that night on the Santa Monica freeway and, since I had broken the axle on my car I just left it at the impound. Considering the condition of that car it was incredible that I even survived that violent accident.

Now in the middle of summer quarter 1985 without transportation, and stuck on campus, I began to get more involved with my course studies. There was a class I was taking that quarter called African-American Literature. A professor, who liked to be called Charles, was teaching the course. I had never met any instructor like him before. For some reason I felt indigenous to what he was teaching. This class afforded me an opportunity to explore the wonderfully gifted authors from the Harlem Renaissance era. Charles was a learned instructor and he was an accomplished musician and poet who had tenure at the black colleges. This brought culture and a renewed sense of identity, much like what Jackie had advocated the previous quarter. He taught with vigor and a determination to get across an awareness. Since his specialty was in English he was an extremely articulate individual. He was also a much traveled man who spoke several languages and possessed a prowess in linguistics.

That course provided me with an opportunity to meet Carrie. She was the only European in that class. She was a beautiful Italian girl and was taking the class as a requirement for graduation. However she seemed comfortable in it and was surprisingly knowledgeable about the subject matter. We formed a friendship which quickly turned into a love affair of unreserved passion. She taught me that interracial intimacy should not be looked down on. Although she was a virtuous, woman what I admired most about Carrie was that she had this way of expressing herself that was unequal to any woman I had previously known. She was very articulate and she became my confidant. I experienced a level of compassion with her unlike I had ever experienced before.

There were many nights when we would lie on the balcony under the moonlight at her house in Hollywood Hills and discuss the world as we knew it to be. She had been given that house by her parents, who had divorced and went on to remarry other people. Carrie was spiritually affected by their separation and I could feel her pain. We were so close that her inner suffering was my distress and visa versa. Carrie was extremely candid about the future of our relationship. She said that her mother would not object, but her father would be devastated by the fact she was dating an African-American man. I respected her candor, which was "righteous" in my eyes. One day Carrie told me that she had to go into the hospital and get a D & C. As smart as I thought I was in those days, I did not know what a D & C was. She told me that it was just some woman problem that needed to be taken care of. I accepted what she said and did not question it since she had never given me any reason to doubt her before. Carrie asked me to come to her house and stay with her the night before she went to have this procedure done. As we lay there in each other's arms, suddenly I heard that little Voice again telling me that something just was not right about all of this. Now, in looking back on that day, I can't help but think that maybe Carrie was terminating a pregnancy. Until this very day I do not know what happened. All I knew was that our relationship was never the same after that and abruptly ended when I proceeded to ask her questions regarding the real reason she had gone to the hospital.

In late summer 1985, one day while preparing dinner for my friend Ginger, I received a call from Johnny B who said that he was leaving Seaside in a few minutes and would be in LA by nighttime. Johnny B had told me on several occasions that he was going to move to LA shortly after I got settled. I hadn't believed him but, this time there was steadfastness in the way he sounded—so I kept an eye out for him.

That night Ginger and I were engaging in a heavy drinking binge. I remember her telling me that she wanted to be my girlfriend because she had never been with a college guy before. Apparently she was intrigued by the fact that I was in college. This was not a sufficient enough reason for me, although I was flattered by her persistence and honestly believed we could have made a great couple. However I was still suffering from the residual effects left by my failed relationship with Carrie, and because of that Ginger never really got a fair chance. We argued about something that had no significance at all. After walking her to her car I noticed a familiar silhouette standing at the bottom of the stairs leading up to my apartment. As I got closer to the contour it became more recognizable. It was Johnny B and suddenly I became the happiest person in the universe. Finally there was one of my true comrades. Never in a million years did I ever think I would be so happy to see him.

We had been friends for a very long time and we had gone

through a lot over the years. We had been in many confrontations with the police. We had been through that press conference on the steps of Seaside City Hall. It was Johnny B who was extremely involved in the campaign to elect me to the Board of Trustees. It was Johnny B who was with me through all the homelessness, drug use and deprivation. And seeing him made me feel somewhat at ease.

Over the years I have had a lot of buddies and they all seem to gravitate around me. I am not sure what their individual motives were for doing this. I suspect that it was partly because I reeked of survival. They knew that wherever I resided there was life in abundance. I accepted their calling, so to speak, and I was adamant about them succeeding in life as well. This made me feel that at least I was doing something right.

Johnny B was from New York and he did not have any of his family members in California. His mother was a prostitute and had died from an overdose of potent heroin when he was just a baby. This compelled him to mature rather quickly, so naturally he was very knowledgeable about life and possessed a spirit that made people like him almost immediately.

Johnny B had become my closest friend over those years in Monterey. Although we argued a lot we had remained very close and I was happy to see him. I asked him how long he intended to be in Los Angeles. He said that he had no intentions of returning to Monterey. I questioned whether there was something that he was running from. He assured me that he, just as I had, wanted to start all over again. He asked could he stay with me for a while. I informed him of the living situation there in the dorms. He understood my dilemma; nevertheless I agreed that he could sleep on the couch until he found a place to live.

Deep inside I knew that this was going to be an indefinite arrangement. He told me that he wanted to use the summer to apply for acceptance into CSULA. He said that he was going to be transferring to CSULA in the fall. Since I was working in the Advisement and Counseling Center and had successfully gone through what he was attempting, I knew exactly the steps to take and I helped Johnny B facilitate that process.

I had never known Johnny B to work and did not expect him to work then. But he surprised me when one day he claimed to have a job. If this was true, I welcomed it because he was putting a strain on me financially—I was basically taking care of both of us for the past few weeks. Sure enough Johnny B had a job working from 11:00 P.M. to 7:00 A.M. loading trucks. Physical labor was not Johnny B's forte so I knew this job would be temporary. Yet I was pleased that Johnny B was making the effort. Since he had to be at work late at night, this left him with a lot of time for hanging around the apartment. I did not feel comfortable about him being around as much as he was because of my roommates, but Johnny B seemed to establish a rapport with them. This was satisfying because I was spending most of my time on the main campus involved in campus activities.

I had become more entangled in Student Government and was considering a run for the presidency when the elections arose the next year. A lot of my efforts on campus evolved around positioning myself for a gallop campaign. Since Johnny B had helped me win the election at MPC I was confident that I would, at least, have a serious chance of winning. The only problem with this positioning was Robert had become my friend and he would be running for re-election. I had this sense of loyalty to him and I did not want to be the one to break that bond. Also there were only seven or eight thousand students at MPC—CSULA had a population of better than twenty-five thousand. This was a different ballgame but I still thought that if I ran I would win.

During those decision-making days in late 1985 I had gradually developed a relationship with Sunshine. He told me that he had been an attorney in the past, specializing in Entertainment Law. Sunshine, to my surprise, was a very intelligent individual. I had heard of his wisdom but our relationship afforded me an opportunity to view this firsthand. He knew more about the Bible than anyone I had met previously in my life. Quickly, I began to understand why Dorothy, Becky and others suggested that we speak, his wisdom was astounding. Sunshine asked me why it had taken so long for me to come and talk with him. There were many days I intended to stop and converse with him and I told him this. I reminded him that I was still relatively new at CSULA and basically wanted to become acclimated with my surroundings. I told him that if I had come and spoken with him previously he may have altered this natural transformation. In the book of Esther the Scripture tells us, "Since it was customary for the king to consult experts in matters of law and justice, he spoke with the wise men who understood the times" (Esther 1:13). He respected my position but still immediately started imparting his God-given wisdom that became so prevalent in my life.

Secularly, Sunshine was in extreme rebellion against the establishment or "The Box" as he referred to it. Apparently his entire life and his accolades were augmented by the wishes of his mother and sister. He told me that even his law degree was a testament to the will of his mother. Although he had been a good attorney he never really wanted to be one in his heart, and dreaded the idea of going back in The Box.

CHAPTER NINE

THE BOX AND DEE DEE FELI

Sunshine told me that all of his life he has wanted to become more in touch with the natural elements. And by the way that he lived, I believed him. Although Sunshine could go home at any moment he chose to live "under the sun." He felt that we all should give freely of those who ask of us and he did. There were rumors that he lived in the basement of the Fine Arts Building. If you asked Sunshine where he lived he would simply say under the sun. Houses, apartments and office buildings represented the box or the establishment he did not want anything to do with.

There were many nights during the late months in 1985 I

would invite Sunshine over to sleep on my couch, but he repeatedly refused. Yet one day he accepted, only to sleep in the cold on the balcony outside. I had developed Agape love for Sunshine. He often quoted Scriptures of wisdom. A lot of the Scriptures he quoted came from the Ecclesiastes and Proverbs books. There were still many people who did not understand him. They felt he was crazy because he would just sit there in the scorching sun for hours. However I had come to know that he was indeed sane—probably more so than most of us. Sunshine assisted me in putting my perplexed life in perspective. Solomon wrote, "For who knows what is good for a man in life, during the few and meaningless days he passes through like a shadow? Who can tell him what will happen under the sun after he is gone?" (Ecclesiastes 6:12). He was the first person who suggested that I attend law school. I did not take his inference seriously then, although as I reflect on his suggestion I believe he definitely planted a seed. Sunshine has remained a very close friend and confidant.

Fortunately the break between the Summer and Fall Quarters was the longest because I needed to go to Seaside and get the rest of my belongings. So I caught the Greyhound there even though I had counted on Johnny B giving me a ride, but he had sold his car one night while on a crack binge.

While in Seaside I stayed at Mel's house. As usual he was out of town. However his companion Fontema agreed to let me stay in a spare room while I was in town. Amazingly, in roughly six months, crack had infiltrated, it seemed, the entire community. My close friends Big James and Ed were now strung out on them. All they talked about was going and getting some. I had never in my life been hooked on any drug. Although I have spent literally thousands of dollars on them, I had always considered drugs a part of socialization and felt that I had some control over them. This dependency that my friends had developed made me feel at ease about my decision to leave Seaside.

Big James agreed to drive me back to Los Angeles if I paid for the gas so I sold my ticket back to Greyhound. We left Seaside in the early morning and for me it would be the last time. Having finally gained a sense of closure to my past, I decided to set my sights on things ahead. This was a sentimentally bitter, but sweet moment. During the drive back to LA we remained conscious of the speed limit because we knew the California Highway Patrol were lurking nearby. The police were constantly looking for reasons to stop people, especially young African-American males. We felt this harassment was in part intended to provoke us into giving the police a reason to use excessive force against us. Realizing this, we would always use extreme caution when driving the freeways. Nonetheless we were still stopped and ordered out of the car and told to stretch out on the ground once again. As they proceeded to search the car they gestured to Big James as to see if he would mind—they never waited for an answer. They said that the reason that they stopped us was that we fitted the description of drug traffickers. And they were looking for drugs and or weapons. They seemed agitated once they did not find anything incriminating.

This antagonistic behavior of the police directed towards African-American males is widely recognized in this country, especially within the African-American communities. It would have been rather asinine of us to carry any drugs. And although we were face down on the ground we managed to keep an eye on the officers' movements. Because it would have been so easy for them to plant some drugs and say they had found them on us. Unfortunately we also knew that there would be no courtroom in America that would have disputed their claim. Paul wrote to the Romans, "But because of your stubbornness and unrepentant heart, you are storing up wrath against yourself for the day of God's wrath, when his righteous judgment will be revealed" (Romans 2:50). We were not only fortunate that they did not plant any drugs but also that they did not beat us, as some cops had tried to do some years ago.

Needing some space to prepare for the Fall Quarter, I asked Johnny B to make himself scarce. He said that he was going to get a room of his own; however that never materialized. He had began to abuse crack and when he got his first financial aid check he spent it on drugs. I did not need or want this around me. I wanted to allow my new roommates the freedom to experience normal dorm living. And I knew the first impression would be the best impression.

At the beginning of fall quarter 1985, Bill hired a new employee named Felicia, or Feli as she preferred to be called. She was a Puerto Rican from the Bronx, New York. She was also a loner and had a sister who lived about 60 miles northeast of Los Angeles. Feli was about 5'8", sandy complexion with brown hair and eyes. She had an hourglass figure and spoke with this strong, provocative New York accent. She was notably articulate and was only eighteen years old when we met.

She and I had extremely different personalities and really did not get along well in the beginning of our relationship. In fact on several occasions she even expressed a genuine dislike towards me—I was not used to this. Although I had never really done anything to her, it was evident that she wanted nothing to do with me other than our working arrangement. Feli would not sit and talk with Dorothy and me about the Bible. Later we found out that she had been raised as a devout Catholic. Yet she was knowledgeable about the Bible and at times even quoted Scriptures.

Feli was probably the most interesting person that I had met in Los Angeles. Up until then Sunshine held that dubious honor. Feli was fluent in both English and Spanish and she was a wizard in mathematics. She was an introvert and somewhat shy until she felt comfortable around you. Although we were not what you would call friends she talked to me a lot and seemed to value my opinion where school issues were concerned. She seemed genuinely intrigued by the fact I had been on my own for so many years. She listened attentively as I told her about my storied past, and I could sense a level of compassion developing between us.

Feli told me that she had left New York at her parents' insistence. Apparently she had become involved with a young man there that had gotten her in some trouble. She said he was sent to Ryker's Island Prison. Her parents felt a change of environment would prove beneficial for her. Feli told me that she did not necessarily want to come to Los Angeles. However because she had an older sister here, this was the only likely place for her to go. Feli's sister was twice her age and they did not have much in common. After finding these things out about each other we realized that we indeed had a lot in common.

Feli also lived in the dorms but, unlike me, she did not necessarily want to experience dormitory life. She preferred the solitude that an off-campus apartment would provide. On numerous occasions she voiced her immense desire to move off campus. Also unlike me, Feli did not possess many independent living skills. She would demurely imply at work that she was hungry. After declining numerous invitations to join me for dinner, one day she surprisingly accepted.

Being renowned for my cooking I wanted to prepare something special for her since it was the first time. I had taken a fancy towards her and was trying to make a positive impression. Feli came over that night and I served stuffed peppers and cabbage. She was surprised that I could cook, so I reminded her that I had been cooking for myself for many years. She thanked me, then left, and I did not know what to expect after that.

Meanwhile, Johnny B had been accepted into CSULA and had begun classes. He asked me if he could stay with me. Apparently he had been staying at Mae's house. I reluctantly agreed to allow him to stay. However, I informed him that I had to speak with my roommates before he moved in. Yet, I did not think that it would be a problem. During the first weeks of the Fall Quarter, my relationship with Feli became fruitful. Dorothy sensed that we were becoming closer and would tease us from time to time. She often joked that I was too old and experienced for Feli—and I should allow her to grow naturally.

Feli had began to come over to my apartment quite frequently in the evenings. We became nightly dinner companions. She would bring her books over and study after eating. She sat for hours upon hours in my room, studying late into the evening. Most nights she fell asleep on my bed and I would just lie there next to her. Gradually, I would hold her into the morning and eventually we made love. We became inseparable and I could not help but think of how we had grown to that point.

All of my partners knew I was in love and it was wonderful. When Yolanda found out about my new girlfriend, for some unknown reason she was displeased. She even went as far as to threaten to break us up. She seemed to be jealous of Feli for some unknown reason. I assured her that Feli posed no threat to our friendship—although Feli did ask me to limit my association with her. During that period I was indifferent to her request and did not take her too seriously.

There were many fall nights when my partners and I would sit in my apartment smoking weed and sometimes cocaine. Feli would be sitting in the back, studying as usual. She did not want to be in there with us and, quite frankly, I did not want her to be in our presence either. She and I smoked weed together on several occasions, but I did not want her to start smoking cocaine. I knew what that drug was capable of doing. She was curious about what I was doing and adamantly blamed a lot of it on my friends. They may have been partly to blame. Feli felt that if I could do with her what I was doing with them, there would be no need for them to be around. She wanted so much for us to just be by ourselves. She felt that if she could get me all by myself, I would concentrate more on my studies. She thought I was smarter than her and would tell me that if she could get straight As—I could too. We finally agreed to start looking for an off-campus apartment.

Christmas was rapidly approaching and the quarter was ending. Of course I received terrible grades that quarter. Feli got straight As and was going back to New York for the holidays. All of my roommates were also spending the holidays at home. I would have the apartment to myself, just as during the other breaks. Feli vowed to return and left for New York right after she took her last final. I was not doing anything special during the holidays so I was looking for something to get into.

There was this girl named Claudette who, like Kev, was from

the Virgin Islands. However, she was from the Island of St. Thomas. She was Yolanda's roommate and had this attraction towards me. However, I felt that this was unwarranted malicious behavior, or female spite motivated by lust after another woman's man. The apostle Paul said, "So I say. Live by the Spirit, and you will not gratify the desires of the sinful nature" (Galatians 5:16). Claudette came over to my apartment on Christmas day and seduced me. She became a constant thorn in Feli's side. However, Feli had this innate ability to deal with stressful situations and throughout our relationship she dealt well with the presence of other women.

Winter Quarter 1986 marked several milestones in my life. That quarter represented my fourth in Los Angeles. I was starting a new job as a Data Processing Clerk in the Alumni Association Office. I had been asked to leave the Advisement office because Bill had told Feli and me that if our relationship became more than just friends, one of us would have to go. So I left because it would be easier for me to find another job on campus than it would have been for her. The Alumni Association office was an interesting place to work. It provided me an opportunity to establish a network consisting of University Alumni professionals. It was while working there I met a woman named Chris. She was an extremely personable, and she taught me about the administrative procedures of operating an office. Under her supervision I must have developed many of my administrative skills.

One wild weekend, in February while on another of my binges, I was kick- boxing with Kev and we all had been drinking a lot. Feli, as usual, did not want to be around us so I had not seen her in a couple of days. After coming down off the high I called Feli and asked her to come over. I informed her that I was not feeling well. Since the beginning of our association Feli had always been extremely protective of me. I had had many girlfriends in the past, but she was the first who seemed to have a legitimate concern for my health. She used to say that someday my body would break down, especially if I continued on those binges. Well, she tried to fix me up, gave me some soup and a massage, staying there holding me the entire night. There had been this extreme pain on the left side of my chest—a discomfort unlike any I had ever experienced before. I thought and hoped it would go away.

However, the next morning the pain was still there even more severe. Feli insisted that we go to the University Health Center. Suddenly I realized that it was difficult even standing. We both knew this was a bit more serious than the common cold. Feli helped me walk up Heartbreak Hill and across campus to the University Health Center. She was literally my crutch and basically did all the walking for both of us.

When we arrived in the Health Center I noticed some tears in her eyes. I knew then that she was indeed in love with me. She said that she was late for a class so I insisted that she go and said that I would see her later. She left reluctantly, vowing to return later to check up on me.

The staff at the Health Center were professional. They made me feel comfortable. The doctor ordered x-rays on my chest and, as I was waiting for the results, I was approached by this rather motherly looking nurse, who introduced herself as Lorraine. I was not aware of it then, but she would become a very special person in my life. She told me that the x-ray negatives were being developed and the doctor would be discussing the results with us shortly.

As she was finishing her comments we noticed Dr. Carblum

coming out of the results room with this rather serious look on his face. We immediately knew that there was indeed something wrong—something very wrong. He asked Lorraine to assist me into the examining room. He proceeded to explain to me in layman's terms that I had a collapsed lung and that it seemed to have been that way for a couple of days, which explained the length of time that I had been in extreme pain. He said that I should have come in much sooner. He told me they did not have the capacity to repair the lung. And then he asked if I knew of someone that would take me to the nearby USC Medical Center. He informed me that if I did not get there soon I could die. This frightened me to the point where I cried. There I was this, self-sufficient tough guy, facing death and all I could think about was those voices of my father telling me things would be different.

Lorraine, sensing that I was in dire need of maternal consoling, instinctively asked where was my family. I explained to her my situation and she automatically assumed the maternal role and called my supervisor Chris, telling her I needed a ride to the USC Medical Center immediately. Suddenly I was on my way, on what could very well had been my final journey.

Upon my arrival at USC Medical Center, which is also the Los Angeles County Hospital, I noticed a huge amount of people. Every barrier we approached was quickly broken down by showing my x-rays. I knew this was serious by the reactions we were getting just by showing those x-rays.

As I sat down in a chair, the lady that brought me there disappeared in the crowd. When she re-emerged there was this team of interns with her, yelling stuff like "priority." They were making me feel very uneasy. Although there had been some hundred people or so already sitting in that emergency room, they rushed me into the treatment room. They put me on a gurney beside this elderly woman who was in cardiac arrest. All of this was happening extremely fast. This doctor, who looked younger than me, introduced himself. He confirmed that my lung was collapsed. And they were going to insert a chest tube to inflate it. He informed me that if the good lung were to stop operating I could die. A nurse was standing there with some consent forms, asking me to sign them, and I did. Then they immediately injected me with a large needle. As they were about to make an incision, I remember a loud beeping sound going off on this machine that was hooked to the elderly lady on the gurney next to me. The entire team that was working on me dropped everything, and joined the team that was working on the elderly woman. I said to myself this is really prioritizing.

As I lay there I witnessed a man being brought into that room who apparently had been shot in the face. All I could see was a lot of cops around him and a lot of blood and open flesh. It was one of the most gruesome scenes I had ever witnessed. An entirely new team surrounded him. I knew that if I was in that room with these people who undoubtedly were facing their mortality, what I was experiencing was serious. The Lord's brother James wrote, "Why, you do not even know what will happen tomorrow. What is your life? You are a mist that appears for a little while and then vanishes" (James 4:14). At that point I became very concerned.

Before I could collect my composure a doctor working on the woman next to me yelled "She's gone." Then, all of a sudden the curtains flew open. However, this time the elderly woman had become a still silhouette with a sheet draped across it. I asked the doctor whether she was dead. He concurred, saying, "That was the fourth today." He warned me that I was about to feel a peculiar sensation in my chest cavity. Almost immediately I felt what he was referring to. He said that it was my collapsed lung inflating.

He informed me they would be moving me to a room as soon as one became available. I joked with him, "I guess I'm going to have to wait until someone else passes for an opening." He smiled and said that he would see me sometime in the near future. He said that I would have to stay in the hospital until my collapsed lung could function on its own. He went on to say that I would be experiencing a lot of pain shortly and gave me something very strong, then he disappeared in the sea of chaos.

About five minutes after I awakened, in the late evening, Feli walked in rather quickly looking as if she had been crying. I told her what had transpired and what the doctors had told me. She cried again and we prayed, talked and laughed together. I told her to leave because she had to catch the bus back to CSULA alone.

The next morning I found Mae, June's mother, and his sisters Renee, Janet and Joyce there. Apparently Feli had called them the night before and informed them of my condition. They were all God-sent and made me feel much better. They were familiar with that ward of the hospital because Mae had been there during her heart surgery a couple of years earlier. This was somewhat of a reunion for her and the nurses. They were there when the doctor came in and told us that if my lung did not heal they would have to operate to correct the problem. All this was confusing, and I inquired whether there was anything I could do to expedite the healing. He told me that I would have to cough up the mucus in my lung so I made this my prime obligation. I wanted to get out of that hospital as soon as possible, because I knew from the days when my father was going in and out of the hospital that the longer I stayed there the more serious the problem was.

Feli came to visit me later that evening. However, this time she bought Johnny B with her and I was pleasantly surprised. This was the first time that he had seen me like this. And I had never seen Johnny B so sentimental, but I could see that he had been crying. He shook his head as to say that all those years of excessive partying had finally caught up with me. Psalms 107:17 tells us, "Some became fools through their rebellious ways and suffered affliction because of their iniquities." He gestured towards me as he was looking at Feli to say she is the one. For the first time I began to seriously consider marrying her. I had not thought that seriously about marrying before. However at that moment I had made up my mind to ask Feli for her hand in marriage. This near-death experience made me view life much differently.

Johnny B said that my roommates had agreed to let him stay there, and I was in no condition to refuse him. He was the one who spoke with my cousin and immediate family by phone. Apparently he had called them in an attempt to re-establish our relationship. He did these things without my requesting him to. He also ate with Feli every night. In fact, those two had become close. And it was Johnny B who kept close care over Feli while I was away. She had become important to him too. And during this downtime Johnny B voluntarily took on most of my responsibilities.

While I was in the hospital I could tell there was something that Feli wanted to tell me. Because I was not in my right mind I began to imagine all sorts of things. I was anticipating that she wanted to tell me that she wanted to move on with her life without me. Over the years I had been a loner and had been left by many women, so my insecurities began to surface. I felt that this was just going to be another one of those situations where I was going to receive the boot. Feli's personality prohibited her from ever saying exactly what she was feeling and I automatically assumed the worst. I remember severely cursing her. She left the hospital that day crying and quite frankly I felt that she had no intentions of ever returning.

Yolanda came to visit me in the interim and was extremely helpful to me in overcoming my fears. She told me that I was a unique individual with a strong past. She said that she was sure that God had a predetermined destiny for me and urged me not to give up. She proclaimed that with God we can do all things. I sensed for the first time that there might have been some hidden feelings there.

While Yolanda was visiting the doctors came in and informed us that they wanted to operate. They said the hole in my lung had not healed on its own so they wanted to operate and repair it. They explained exactly what they wanted to do and why. All this complicated the matter further, and they wanted me to sign some more consent forms. I told them that I was not ready to sign any more forms. And they said that they would give me some time to think about it, but they also advised me that I only had two choices, and one of them included the possibility of death.

After hearing this Yolanda immediately suggested that there was only one decision to make, that I consent and be operated on as soon as possible. I was really afraid and instructed Yolanda to ask Feli, who had not been to the hospital in a couple of days, to come and see me. I really wanted to discuss this delicate situation with her. Yolanda reluctantly agreed.

Feli came to see me the next day just as the doctors were making their rounds. She said that this was my decision; however she conceded that if this was her decision to make she would have the operation. She also assured me that she was going to be there throughout this entire ordeal. I signed the release forms and the doctors said they were going to operate the following morning. Feli left and we knew that the next time we would see each other would be in the post-operative period.

Between the time that I signed those forms, until they came to pick them up, I remained deliberately awake. This was the first time that I had been in a situation such as this. I could not help but think of my mortality. I was thinking of all the sinful stuff that I had done in my life—and was wondering was this repayment for all the wrong I had done in my life. I could not help but hear those desperate outcries to my parents when I was a child. However, this time there were no answers—especially from my parents. In actuality there was nobody but me. This was a profoundly isolated period in my life that seemed to last an eternity.

I was afraid and could feel Feli was too, although she didn't say so. I began to think about a lot of things, such as what exactly had been my purpose on earth. I was unsure for the first time. I could not think of one accomplishment. The single greatest accomplishment to date was the day I was accepted into the University system. And what had all that gained me? Especially if I were to die. I began to think about the fact that I was the last surviving male in my generation with no offspring. I began to think of the women in my past who had gotten abortions at my insistence, so that I would not have the responsibility of raising a child. And what about the drugs I had sold people over the years? What about the harm I had done to myself? Would God forgive me?

Although the doctors said that there was a 90% chance that I would come through this operation alive, I only concentrated on the 10% chance that I would not. Finally I dozed off to sleep, only to be awakened by the nurse telling me there were three people in the waiting room for me. She reminded me that I was extremely blessed and that I should consider myself fortunate. She told me that there were two ladies and a gentleman waiting for me. I knew that it could only be Feli, Yolanda and Johnny B. I remembered the nurse trying to ease my noticeable fears and joking with me about my sexual endowment as they were putting a mask on my face.

The next thing I remember I was waking up and Feli was smiling in my face. It was a victorious, joyful occasion, considering I was alive. I asked her whether the operation had taken place and she informed me that it had. With adoration she proclaimed that it had been successful. She told me not to speak and to just rest. Then she ran to inform the nurse that I had regained consciousness.

Later that day the doctors came in and showed me exactly what they had done. They felt that I had been born with a blob on my lung. They said that they did not think that any drugs and/or alcohol had contributed to my misfortunes. This made us feel somewhat relieved, because in our hearts we felt the problem was either caused by my long history of alcohol and drug use, or, was the result of Kev and me kick-boxing. He may have broken my rib, causing a puncture to my lung. However, the doctors assured us that my punctured lung was not the due to any unnatural occurrence.

During my recovery the nurses informed me that there had been a little argument between Feli and Yolanda. Apparently the doctor had told the three that there could only be one person with me during my initial recovery. The nurse said that both Yolanda and Feli vehemently debated for the right to be there. Yolanda argued on the premise that she was my surrogate sister, and Feli took the position of the significant other. The debate was settled when I apparently woke briefly in the post-operative room and yelled Feli's name.

Feli was there everyday after that. She was concerned somewhat about dosages of drugs the doctors were giving me for pain. The doctors told me this would be the case. They were giving me large shots of morphine every four hours and massive amounts of codeine every two hours. I began to like this and immediately thought about "Champ," who had been in Vietnam. He used to tell us about morphine and its addictive effects, and now I was experiencing what he had warned me about. This made Feli very uncomfortable. She even went to the doctors against my will and implored them to gradually wean me off of the drugs.

Several days later the nurse told me that I had a telephone call. She did not say who it was, but when I answered the phone I was greeted by an unfamiliar voice. The lady on the other end was an Insurance Investigator. Apparently my mother had taken a life insurance policy out on me the day that I went into the hospital. She asked me a few questions and then said good-bye.

I am not sure how I was feeling at that point, especially since my mother had not called to check on my condition. Feli came in later and we talked about the telephone call. She could feel my distress and those moments brought us closer. She knew the Agape I had for my family and sympathized with my incompleteness in that area. She seemed to divinely know exactly what it was I needed to hear, then.

The doctor came in and said that I was ready to leave. So the next morning, with Feli's shoulder as a crutch, I did. We went reluctantly back to the dorms and Feli suggested that I stay with her because she could take better care of me so I agreed. The reception I received was very supportive. My friends had apparently gone to the hospital and given blood. They all seemed very anxious for me to get well and showed a legitimate concern.

Feli and I began to look for another place as I was recovering. We had gained several friends while I was going through my ordeal. Lorraine, the nurse, and her friend Connie, also a nurse in the Health Center, had taken it upon themselves to adopt us. Both would stop by the dorms with food and medicine. They made these house calls on numerous occasions and we both welcomed them.

There was this Armenian girl that I knew from my Business classes. She had an apartment in the Mariannas which was walking distance from CSULA. She was transferring to Pepperdine University in Malibu and wanted someone to buy her out of a lease. She gave us an offer we could not refuse. We went over and liked what we saw. It was small, with one bedroom, one bath, a kitchen and a living room. Since we both liked solitude it was perfect. We made an appointment to go in and speak with the manager. An odd thing happened as we were closing the deal. Just as we were about to sign the lease, Feli pulled out but I didn't and signed. She later told me that she was unsure what a lease was and what our obligation would entail. I did not mind that she did not sign the lease and although, in theory, the apartment was mine I assured Feli that the apartment was really ours.

I sat the Spring Quarter out and really did not go on campus often. However, my court date was rapidly approaching. This concerned my automobile accident some months earlier. I knew that I was in for a stern punishment. Because I had had three other driving convictions in the past, I was aware that there was a mandatory county jail term in my immediate future. We were hoping the judge would be lenient and only give me probation. But still, we knew there was a strong probability that I would be spending time incarcerated.

Nonetheless, we went to traffic court that day overly optimistic. The Judge suspended my driver's license for two years. He also sentenced me to serve sixty days in the Los Angeles County Jail. The look on Feli's face told it all, she was devastated and the security she felt in our relationship was shattered. Suddenly I knew why she did not want her name on the lease. I now understood why she had been concerned about our living situation, and during the entire time that we were living at the Mariannas she had not given up her apartment on campus. The Judge did, however, give me a sixty-day stay of execution. This allowed me some time to make arrangements for my apartment. Feli had made it clear that she was not going to stay in that apartment without me. She had previously mentioned on several occasions that after the quarter had ended she was going to move with her sister to Canyon Country.

Feli began to act sort of strange and I was becoming leery

of her. She told me one day that she was pregnant and that she was afraid if she told her family they would disown her. I assured her that she indeed would be a part of my life forever. However, I was going to jail and she was as certain about my future as she about hers. She informed me of her intention to terminate the pregnancy. I beseechingly begged her not to, however to no avail. I really did not put forth much resistance. As I look back at that dark moment in my past I am sorry not only for myself, but also for Feli, because I honestly was neglecting my duties as a man to sufficiently manage that delicate situation. Or maybe both of us were spiritually oblivious.

Shortly afterwards our relationship began to deteriorate rapidly. I went back to wasting time with my destructive cohorts. We continued to use drugs, and at one point I became so furious at Feli for not giving me money to buy cocaine that I destroyed some of her valuables. Feli seemed at the point in time lost, very lost because her only friend, me, had betrayed her. I had become a monster, a stranger, a walking demon, possessed by the demonic sprits. "For our struggle is not against flesh and blood, but against the rulers, against the authorities, against the powers of this dark world and against the spiritual forces of evil in the heavenly realms" (Ephesians 6:12). She, just like many others, no longer knew me. I was trapped inside of someone I no longer knew. What I did know was that I was consumed inside myself, struggling to escape the inevitable.

The quarter ended and, as expected, Feli's sister came over one day in mid June 1986 and we loaded her belongings in the back of the van. We passionately kissed, before they boarded the van and slowly drove away. I could see Feli staring at me through the back window. She had indeed left. Although Feli had told me that she was leaving because her sister was expecting a baby soon, deep inside I felt that she was not exactly prepared for the commitment that our relationship presented. This was evident after she had refused to put her signature on the lease agreement. Yet still, Feli was my closest confidant, my lover and my best friend. We did everything together and when she left I really felt incomplete for awhile. The day she left, I went back into that apartment and the entire place felt sort of empty. Feli had put her stamp of femininity on that atmosphere. I am unsure how to explain the emotions vibrating through my very soul after she left.

CHAPTER TEN

CORRUPTION AND CONFUSION

The post-Feli era proved to be extremely confusing. During the early summer 1986 days I sort of dove in to the refuge that my buddies provided. I knew Feli was just a phone call away, but it just was not the same. I believed her when she promised to return in the fall. This would have provided me with the sixty days I needed to serve my forthcoming jail sentence.

I had made arrangements to turn myself into the Los Angeles County Jail. The court had agreed to allow me to participate in the Work Furlough Program. This would give me an opportunity to work, take classes and serve time simultaneously. However the program cost $100 a week, which I did not mind paying if

I would not have to sit in a jail cell all day. I had heard much about the infamous, very volatile Los Angeles County Jail and frankly was in no hurry to go there.

During Summer Quarter 1986 I started working with Fred in the Testing Center. Lav, the boss, had hired me just before I turned myself in. He was a very hyperactive person who seemed to do everything rather briskly. He understood the dilemma that I was in and wanted to help me as much as he could. The people at the court had told me that I would be in custody for about 48 hours. Apparently this was the amount of time that was needed to transfer me to the Biscaluz Facility where they housed the Work Furlough inmates in East Los Angeles. That facility was right around the corner from my apartment and right down the street from CSULA. So this would be the ideal location for me to serve my sixty days.

After turning myself in I remember this large deputy belligerently demanding that we all strip naked. The in-processing took about 15 hours. I had limited knowledge of "Jail House Culture" from my associations on the streets. I knew that I would only be there for a short period of time and made a point of not talking too much. However in the jail system you have to boast a little in the initial stages, because if you don't the other inmates might view you as weak and try to use you to make a name for themselves. I realized that I was being inaugurated into a system that lacked rocket scientists or people with academic prowess. So I assumed that my book knowledge, added to my common and street senses, would provide me with the necessary tools to successfully complete my jail tenure.

Finally after twenty-four hours or so on the 9000 floor at LA County Jail, I was told by several inmates that the next stop for us would be where we would serve our time. I remember specifically 9500 ward where all inmates go while awaiting classification. There were massive amounts of inmates—black inmates consolidated with other black inmates, Mexican inmates consolidated with other Mexican inmates, and white inmates, as few as there were, consolidated with other white inmates. The Asians sort of hung with the blacks. Suddenly I understood what I had heard about jail being a segregated environment. Nonetheless I continued to listen for my name over the intercom because I would be transferring to Biscaluz Center within a day.

On the bus ride to the Biscaluz Center we passed directly in front of my apartment. Kev was watching my place and I knew that within the next couple of days I would be returning there, at least during the day. The Probation Officer who was assigned to my case was an African-American woman. I felt somewhat at ease because of this. And I was extremely confident that I would successfully complete this program. The Probation Department was unaware of the proximity of my apartment to the center and it would have been impudent of me to tell them that I lived within walking distance.

The inmates slept at the Biscaluz Center every night. Every morning we were released, approximately one hour before we were to be at work. We were prohibited to indulge in any type of drugs or alcohol. If we violated those decrees we were sent back to the Main County jail. And they would recalculate your time and deem you ineligible for further participation in the Work Furlough Program.

In the mornings I would leave the center and stop by my apartment, shower, eat and sometimes go back to sleep. The Testing Center was a very laid-back environment—Lav wanted it that way. He was more like my peer than my supervisor. We partied together. After extensive stays in the Pub, my co-workers would advise that I go home and rest, because they knew that I had to be back at the Biscaluz Center by 7:00 P.M.

One day, while at work, I was going downstairs to get a drink and I ran into my Probation Officer coming up the stairs. She apparently was coming to check if I was where I was supposed to be. Since I was, she expressed her confidence that I would complete the program. I knew that my indiscretions would eventually catch up with me. However I was out of control, being guided by a force much stronger than me.

One afternoon at school I met two "Nubian Princesses" named Pam and Tonia. And we all immediately formed a very amicable alliance. They were extremely prayerful people and invited me to join their prayer group in the evenings. I really wanted to, mostly because their persistence reminded me of Cynthia O and Phyllis when they were trying to get me to convert to Buddhism. Yet there was a big difference, Pam and Tonia were both devout Christians. Pam was Pentecostal and Tonia was a Baptist—I could relate to the latter. Because of my obligation to Biscaluz I requested a "rain check." As I left their presence I remember hearing that Voice once again, this time telling me that those two young ladies would become special in my life and indeed they did. It was immediately evident that they were truly remarkable people so I agreed to meet them the next day for prayer.

Earlier that day Connie had asked me to come by the Health Center to get some cough drops for a cold I had. I did, and left vowing to come and chat with her in the very near future. When I got back to the Biscaluz Center that evening, everything seemed normal. It just so happened it was the evening my Probation Officer was conducting intake interviews. Normally, I would just go straight to bed but I wanted to be cordial and decided to walk by the window to acknowledge her. She demanded that I come closer. I concurred because that particular day I had had nothing to drink or ingested any drugs and felt comfortable going closer to her.

She immediately insisted that she smelled alcohol and asked whether I had been drinking. I told her that I had not and informed her that it was probably the cough drops that she was smelling. And it was, nevertheless, she did not believe me and asked the deputies at the facility to "roll me up." They did, although with minimal resistance from me.

When we got to the holding tanks on the other side of the facility, I was still contesting their decision to roll me up. Apparently one of the officers became irritated and grabbed me from behind and administered the infamous deadly "choke hold." When I regained consciousness I was in a holding tank, about to be transferred back to the Main County Jail. In the squad car I figured out what was really going on. This playing field was unlike any other that I had been on in my entire life. At that moment I understood finally what people had been warning me about when they said that jail is easy to get into, but hard to get out of.

A few hours later, when I was back in 9500 ward, they informed me during classification that an additional thirty days had been added to my sentence. This was a normal punishment for inmates rolled up from a particular program. After that they sent me to the "hole" for a week, feeding me "Juke Balls" twice a day. Juke Balls are compressed leftover food from the chow hall. Once back in a cell on "mainline," I remember an inmate trustee coming around with a pad and pen. He was asking inmates what was their commitment offense. Apparently he was screening possible participants in the Work Release Program. In my opinion this program was better than Work Furlough. A participant in this program would have to come to the Main County Jail at 6:00 A.M. and work for the grounds officer for the amount of days you have to serve in custody. Even though I was eligible for the program I did not feel they would allow me to participate in it because of what happened to me in the Work Furlough Program.

However, after a couple of days I was called down for an interview. They asked me some questions and quite frankly gave me the impression that they were not going to choose me. They indicated that if indeed they were to consider me that I would know by noon the next day. The next day came and it was about 1:00 P.M. and I had not heard my name. But about 1:30 P.M. my name was called over the intercom. Shortly after, I was released on the Work Release program before 3:00 P.M. that afternoon and I was elated. This enabled me to go back to my normal routine. At the Testing Center I was relegated to working as a proctor on the weekends, which was a small price to pay for freedom. An officer told me one morning the county jail system was so accommodating because of the large volume of inmates in the county jail during those years. Judging by the overcrowding of the cells, I understood exactly what he meant because we were sleeping eight men deep in a cell designed for four people.

I was adamant about successfully completing the Work Release Program because I did not want to go back behind bars.

Since I was able to sleep at home I spent a lot of time with my friends and attended evening classes. One evening, while partying with friends, I got to bed extremely late and called into the program sick. We were told that we were allowed to miss one day. However that day would have to be made up at the end of your term.

When I returned the following Monday the officers instructed me to turn around and put my hands behind my back. I knew that command represented the end of my participation in the Work Release Program. There I was once again sitting in a holding tank, waiting to be processed yet another time, into the main county jail. This time it went very quickly and I was on the 9000 floor within the hour.

I was transferred to Wayside Ranch to serve an additional sixty days. There I worked as a clerk in the Program office. They assigned me to the fire camp dorm which was sort of a privilege. I knew that I would be there for a while and attempted to become as acclimated to my surroundings as possible. No one knew where I was so I did not expect to receive any letters. I told Kev my situation so he could keep a watch out on my apartment again.

I witnessed a lot of evil during my incarceration—mostly violent racial confrontations. However it is protocol in the penal system to just turn your head, especially if its nothing to do with you or your "homeboyz." Because of the volatility of the vehement penal system, you must remain aware of your surroundings. Anything can happen at any moment. Fortunately I served that sixty days rather incident-free. When I returned home everything was just as I had left it.

Unfortunately I had no job or money and was behind in my rent payments. Even though I had had to start over before, this was different because I was virtually depressed about my situation and lacked motivation. Never before had I felt so drained. Frankly, I needed stimulation to conjure up strength. 1 Samuel 14:7 tells us, "Do all that you have in mind," his armor-bearer said. "Go ahead; I am with you heart and soul."

In the past whenever I found myself in that situation I would go to the welfare office for immediate assistance. Also I knew that I could get an emergency loan from the financial aid office. I did both. I had gotten an Eviction Notice while I was in jail. And I was not aware of how exactly to deal with this. So I went to the Legal Aid Society and they showed me how to file a Response to an Unlawful Detainer—which gave me an additional 60 days to come up with the necessary funds.

In the meantime I had met a neighbor named Cliff. He had been living in the Mariannas for a long time. He was a veteran of the Vietnam war. We became good friends in a short period of time partly because he seemed to understand me. I believe he could appreciate the fact that I was resilient and an overcomer. He said to me on several occasions that he appreciated the fact that I seemed to persevere despite the short- comings in my life. He said that I did not blame my circumstances on anyone, and I just sort of dealt with adversity. Nonetheless, Cliff told me that if there would ever come a time when I had taken it as far as I could go in terms of keeping my apartment, that I could sleep on his couch for a couple of days. This was an extremely good gesture considering we had not known each other long. And I am sure today that upright gesture was the catalyst for our fruitful relationship.

On campus I was using the Testing Center phone to call Feli in New York. She had been gone a long time and it was becoming evident that she was not coming back as she had promised. I began subconsciously to move forward in my life without her. Her cousin had told me that Feli had begun to use drugs rather frequently. She went on to say that Feli wasn't like this before she came to California. Since I was the closest to her for the entire time that she was in Los Angeles, her parents felt that I was responsible for this unfortunate change in her life. As much as I wanted to, I could not dispute their claim, because up until Feli had met me she was a quiet, introverted, and homely girl, although she had had some covert unfavorable adventures with that guy she grew up with in the Bronx. However I knew that she had never experienced that dark side that was so prevalent in my life during those times. Yet I also knew that I had just lost the most important person in my life.

Most of what was occurring in my life in late 1986 and early 1987 was spontaneous. No single incident was congenial, although I had begun to spend more time with Pam and Tonya. My confidants at CSULA became more refined. There were specific topics that I would discuss with certain people. Pat, an Administrator on campus, had taken a meticulous interest in me. She and Connie were good friends and each of them were intricate parts of the network that I had unknowingly established. There were others in that network, Ralph Dawson and Drs. Taylor and Carter. They all had become surrogate members of my family, there to help me rebound from this deprivation.

In early 1987 I had landed a job with a New York Stock Exchange brokerage firm located in downtown Los Angeles. Faheen, a beautiful and sexy Arabian virtuosi, deemed me qualified to be a Margins clerk. This was an extremely high security job and well paying. This job would afford me an opportunity not only to learn about the stock market, but moreover and equally important it would provide the means for me to keep my apartment. But still, deep inside I wanted to leave that apartment because of the memories.

In February 1987 I decided to call Margarita. We had kept in touch and she was glad to hear from me. Coincidentally, she would be coming to Los Angeles soon on business with her mother. Of course I invited her to stay with me at my apartment and she gladly accepted and I anxiously prepared for her arrival. Since my telephone had been disconnected I asked her to contact me at my neighbor's.

Margarita called me at my neighbor's when she arrived in Los Angeles. She would be spending that first night at the hotel with her mother. However the next morning she would be driving across town to my place. I gave her directions but she never arrived, nor did I receive a call. When we spoke next she was back in Salinas. Apparently she had gotten lost on the freeway; we were both very disappointed. She had not called because she did not want to disturb my neighbors. I was devastated over this because I knew deep inside that she was coming to scout the territory. We often talked about her joining me one day in Los Angeles. As I reflect on that period I believe that if we had spent that time together we would have united. Unfortunately that was also the determinate lost opportunity. To this very day I have never seen Margarita again.

Early one morning I was awakened by a familiar brawny knock on the door. It was LAPD. I knew that they were not coming to evict me because I had a pending court date concerning that matter. Apparently, they were looking for me because Johnny B had given them my name. He had been picked up about 3:00

A.M. on a corner in South Central. He was allegedly under the influence of a controlled substance and was wearing nothing but boxer shorts. He had a club in his hand and had been yelling "Bam, Bam!" Apparently he was having hallucinations and delusions, stimulated by his fascination with the Flintstones cartoon character, and caused by "Acute Cocaine Intoxication." This bothered me immensely because other than Feli there was no one closer to me than him.

Mae often told me that I was the influential figure of our core group. She said since I was the only one who always had money, it was me who facilitated their drug habits. Although Johnny B had started to live with her in South Central, she, Johnny, and her sons, would seek refuge around me. She said that their will power was not equal to that of mine. She went on to imply that they were not functional drug addicts like I was at that time. "'For the lips of a priest ought to preserve knowledge, and from his mouth men should seek instruction-because he is the messenger of the Lord Almighty. But you have turned from the way and by your teaching have caused many to stumble: you have violated the covenant with Levi,' says the Lord Almighty" (Malachi 2:7,8). She said that their lifestyles were not conducive with mine and I should not have allowed them to be around me. And just as Feli's parents had, she too, held me responsible for Johnny B's misfortune. In a lot of ways I understood what she was talking about and in certain terms she was correct in her assumption.

The police wanted to release Johnny B to my care and I concurred. We got in touch with his family in Delaware and arranged a flight for him back there. Johnny B left Los Angeles and I have never seen or heard from him since. I assume his family put him into a drug rehabilitation program. That is what he wanted because in his soul he did not want to do drugs anymore. We would talk often about changing our lifestyles. We knew there would eventually be consequences to the way that we had been living. We examined our lifestyles minutely when our friend Rico's body wasted away slowly, painfully and eventually he died from AIDS. We had been living on the edge for a very long time. Now I was having another unfortunate enlightenment, viewing destruction up close and personal. However it never quite affected me this way. Yet I did know if I continued to live the way that I was living, this could happen to me. Or, maybe even worse.

My mother called and told me that my brother was getting married. They had set a date in mid-July. He had not included me in his wedding plans and they assumed that I did not want to come. My brother and I had not spoken in a few years and this had an adverse effect on me. When we spoke I wished him well in his new life with Loretta, who is a beautifully spirited person, if a bit on the spoiled side. He inquired whether I would be attending. After explaining to him my financial situation he offered to pay a portion of the cost of a ticket. Graciously my mother and sisters offered to pay a portion of the price. They sent me a ticket and took a couple of days off of work and flew to Richmond.

I was feeling somewhat apprehensive about returning to Richmond for the first time since the early 80s. Frankly, I was having second thoughts about going. However I did go and it was surprisingly a nice visit. I had not seen any of my cousins in a long time and this afforded me that opportunity.

While in Richmond I met a young woman by the name of

Amanda. She was a devout Christian girl who sang in the church choir with my siblings. I had not known her before I left home and she was a few years younger than me. However we took a liking to each other and discussed the Lord extensively. She testified how God had been the center of her life and He should receive all the glory for the replenishment in our lives. She reminded me of my spiritual rearing. The entire time that I was home I was experiencing mixed emotions. I could not avoid recognizing how the environment had changed. Suddenly I realized something about myself. I had become a Californian. In most ways this visit brought a sense of closure for my recurring homesickness.

Back in Los Angeles, at work, Faheen called me into her office. There were two distinguished looking gentlemen in there with her. She introduced them as Credit Card Fraud Investigators. I knew that I had never owned any credit cards in my life so I was relieved that they could not have been there specifically for me. However they asked whether I knew a gentleman by the name of Dumas. I acknowledged that I did. They said that he had put my name and job location and number on a credit card application. They explained that they were investigating Dumas for fraud. I explained to them that Dumas was just an acquaintance that I knew from CSULA, and I had no knowledge that he had used me as a credit reference. They showed me copies of the application and explained what exactly were the penalties that Dumas was facing. This was a serious matter. They advised me that because of the nature of my job I should limit my association with people like Dumas. I assured them that I would.

After those men left, I noticed Faheen and the other managers in a meeting. Eventually they invited me in. When I walked into that office the atmosphere alarmed me, this was not going to be a friendly meeting. They reminded me about a clause in my contract that specifically stated that I could not participate in, or be involved with, any fraudulent activities. I explained to them that I had no knowledge of Dumas' business activities. They insinuated that it would be in the best interest of the company if I would resign. I asked them if I did not quit, what next. They assured me that they would indeed fire me. Since there existed no alternative I reluctantly resigned.

In late summer, again, without a job, I knew that I would eventually lose my apartment. The money I was making with the Testing Center was not sufficient to maintain it, I knew that homelessness was imminent. I began to prepare myself for the worst. There were places I could go, but pride prohibited me from asking for help.

On campus Becky had left work on maternity leave and I was spending more time with Tonya and her family, also Pam had started to hang around me. And I was also spending more time with Renee, one of June's older sisters. Yolanda had disappeared and no one knew exactly where she was, although my heart was telling me that she was all right.

My court date, for yet another unlawful detainer hearing arrived. I had become proactive concerning these proceedings and paid careful attention to the testimony. The owner of the apartments perjured herself under oath. She was exposed after I asked her the date she had served me the notice of eviction. I could prove that I was incarcerated on that date. I had anticipated her doing this. Ultimately the Judge correctly ruled in my favor and I was given an additional ninety days rent free. This would allow me the necessary time to get the money together to move.

CORRUPTION AND CONFUSION

Inwardly that Voice was telling me to move back to the dorms. There at least I would be comfortable. But my pride did not allow me to do that either. So after saving some money, I moved into a hotel in an upscale downtown neighborhood. Almost immediately I found myself a streetwalker, late at night. There are many late night streetwalkers in downtown Los Angeles. Even though I did not necessarily have to be out there, I strangely was. Probably I was out there because of the crack. Once again I was a moderate user and it was out there in large affordable amounts. I had paid my rent through Welfare so all excess money went on drugs and alcohol.

Eventually I got a job as a data entry clerk with a company that made and sold gear for police and firemen. Ironically a person who had very little respect for law enforcement now was working for the very company that made police gear. The company was Jewish-owned, and employed almost exclusively Mexican illegal immigrants. I worked closely with the payroll clerk and I viewed the books often.

In fact the owner Harold encouraged it, because the more versatile I became the more valuable to the company I was. Even though that company had massive sales, I was getting paid peanuts compared to what others were making doing the same thing I was. That company was extremely solvent because there was virtually no competition in the area. Since he was only paying the Mexican shop workers minimum wages, I can only imagine how much he was clearing. I was disturbed by this because I had read about "sweat shops" before. However until then I had never had the opportunity to view one firsthand. Instead of trying to make conditions better for the workers in the shop, I concentrated on making my personal finances better. I listened to

Harold carefully and he taught me every aspect of that business. Although I knew that he was not necessarily teaching me the business so he could promote me in the future, he was teaching me his business so that there would be no position in the administrative division that I could not do.

He would always boast to his associates that he had an astute college student working for him. Sure enough there came a point in time when I indeed knew every aspect of Harold's business. He had even given me access to a safe where he kept only useless rubber stamps. However one day I noticed a single one dollar bill in plain view. Undoubtedly this was a test of my integrity. He did not know it then but unknowingly he was creating an adversary. I was already resentful of him because of the wages he was paying those hard-working shop employees. His customers would complain about the high prices. He could do this because he knew that he was in possession of a monopoly. A few days later, while I was assisting a police officer with his purchase, the officer inquired whether there was a way he could get a discount. I informed him that I did not think so. He then insisted that surely there must be a way. I knew what he was insinuating and pondered for a minute while he was trying on his clothes.

Harold was very shrewd and I knew what he was capable of doing. Based on the safe incident, I felt this could very well be another of his loyalty tests. I also knew from my past experiences not to trust police officers. I knew how low they would go. So I weighed the advantages and the disadvantages on whether I should sell this large amount of merchandise to this corrupt cop.

Since I was a risk taker I nodded to the officer as he was

coming out of the dressing room. He seemed to comprehend what I intended. When we went to the check-out counter I only rang up an amount about one fifth of the actual retail amount of his purchase. He recognized that he was saving over $200, afterward I helped carry his bags to his car where he gave me a $100 bill. I informed him that if we were to do any more business he would have to be more generous next time. He then gave me another twenty dollar bill and suddenly we had established a very cordial, fruitful business relationship. He said that he had some more friends that might be interested in my services and assured me that our business would remain confidential.

Since Harold had taught me all of the aspects of his business so well, this job became very profitable for me. Often I would leave that place with close to $1000 daily. I do not think Harold knew; in fact, I know that he did not because if he had known he would not have allowed this to go on. His other trusted employees would joke about the amount of in-house theft that was going on in that place. Apparently I was not the first employee to do that in his company. The Scripture warns us, "Whoever loves money never has money enough; whoever loves wealth is never satisfied with his income. This too is meaningless" (Ecclesiastes 5:10). Harold was an extremely wise individual. However in many ways he was naïve, in that he used his wisdom in a way that proved to be detrimental to the disadvantaged and the oppressed immigrants and minorities that worked for him.

One morning, while in my room on the 12th floor preparing for work, the building started vibrating, the floor under me felt as if I was walking on a soft mattress. When the window I was standing next to shattered out of the frame, I had to grab hold of the television to keep from falling out. Once again my mortality flashed before my very eyes. As the shaking slowed and as I was running down the fire escape, I remember passing all of these beautiful naked people. There were many unashamed people in the raw standing in the middle of the streets of downtown Los Angeles. The luminous stares of those nude people, having escaped their deaths, is a sight that will forever remain engraved in my memory. Although I had experienced earthquakes before, I had never been in one twelve floors up. It was truly the single most terrifying experience that I had ever had. If that building had collapsed I would have undoubtedly been killed. But still I knew that Harold would be conducting business as usual and went to work.

    I saw on the evening news that the earthquake had hit CSULA pretty hard. Apparently it had caused a large section of concrete to collapse, killing a young Asian freshman. For a long period of time Salazar Hall, where they housed business courses, was closed for repairs. This made it very hectic for the business students to get our needed classes. Many of the classes were temporarily held in King Hall where the Social Sciences classes were held. This enabled us to converse with the more philosophically-minded students on campus. Fortunately the earthquake enlightened me about the structure of that hotel. Obviously it was not a secure, sturdy building so I immediately started to look for another place.

    Tania helped me find another, inexpensive place to move in. However I was leery of the location of the room. It was in the McArthur Park District. Although I did like the room and the manager, the area was notorious for drug dealers and drug addicts. However I was willing to tolerate that censured environment in order to get out of the Milner so I reluctantly moved into that room and soon became content.

Tania and Pam agreed to occasionally drive me around to seek another place that would be more conducive. The apostle Paul wrote to the Romans concerning Priscilla and Aquila, "They risked their lives for me. Not only I but all the churches of the Gentiles are grateful to them" (Romans 16:4). I was cognizant that they were being accommodating because they wanted very much for me to go to church with them. It was extremely fulfilling to know that at least there was someone who cared about my spiritual development.

Soon after that day I went to work intoxicated. Harold was overwhelming me with responsibilities and I had secretly begun to train this young seamstress how to use a computer. As I was showing her how to use a software application, Harold walked in. He became notably agitated that I was teaching her to do something other than sew. He impudently ordered her back into the shop, as if implying that she was out of place. This reminded me of institutionalized slavery so I promptly went to Harold's office to question his actions. He belligerently demanded that I get out of his face. His indignant tone was inappropriate and I warned him not to ever address me in that tone again. As I began to walk away he called me "nigger" and pushed me in the back. I turned around and slapped him in the face, he hit the ground and I remember this scream. It was the elderly Jamaican woman who had worked there with Harold for twenty-five years. Suddenly, three firemen that were shopping in the store ran back into the office area and grabbed me. They detained me until the police arrived.

Harold asked that they not arrest me because he was afraid that I might retaliate in some way. I was cited for battery and was given a court date. When I went to court I thought that the Judge was going to sentence me to spend time in jail. However the public defender informed me that she and the DA had agreed to drop the charges if I would pay for Harold's broken eyeglasses, also I could not go near his place of business again. She said that once that restitution was paid, this infraction would be removed from my record. I had never known Harold to wear any glasses but those already broken ones he wore everyday. His glasses had been broken since the day that I met him. It seems a person such as Harold needed the satisfaction of knowing that he had control over the situation. By his getting some new glasses out of this ordeal, he felt as if he was coming out ahead or winning in some distorted way. I had heard about people such as he before in my life and now I was experiencing it with my own eyes.

There I was, once again jobless, and as always when I was in that predicament I turned to the bottle. By then I had made that natural progression from beer to wine. Most of the time I would not even go to school and was becoming just as functionless as my partners. Tania continued to come over and take me to church with her. She could tell from my etiquette that I had been inside many Baptist churches in my life. She was beginning to feel that there was promised destiny for our relationship. Inadvertently this motivated me to do something significant about my condition.

My mentor Connie had suggested that I not always concentrate my job search efforts on campus. She reminded me that there was a big world out there and numerous jobs just waiting for a guy such as myself. This made sense and I focused on employment off campus. Amazingly I was almost immediately hired by an advertising company to work as a clerk in the accounting department. This was one of the highest-paying jobs I had ever held. Tania attributed this blessing to my being obedient to the Lord. Her proclamation was true in the sense that I was making an attempt to be obedient. Nonetheless I began to apply myself.

I made it a point to get to work on time and leave late. Since I was the only African-American male working there I knew that I was probably filling a quota mandated by Federal and State Affirmative Action Laws. But I felt that my job performance would eventually prove me invaluable. I remember this one particular woman walking past me on several occasions making comments such as "Boy, are you still here?" She would warn that my employment there was only temporary and that the management had made a mistake in hiring me. I sort of just ignored her comments because I needed that job badly.

After only a week, sure enough, the personnel manager called me into her office. She said that they had made a mistake in hiring me and that I was fired. I did not get any other explanation than that. Inside my soul I knew I was terminated because I'm black, this was an atrocity. She assured me that I would be receiving my final check via express mail, as if that was some consolation.

When I received that check I put two weeks rent inside of an envelope and mailed it to my landlord. The rest I wasted on alcohol. I remember I had two dollars and twenty-five cents leftover. It was about 12:30 A.M. and I decided to walk to this burrito truck and spend the two dollars. I remember asking two ladies in passing for change for a quarter. I was going to call Tania and talk, I did not want to spend the entire quarter because

I knew I was going to need that nickel the next day. Shortly after that I remember a policeman stopping me and asking where had I put the weapon. I asked them what were they talking about. They pointed toward those two women I had just passed and said that they had told them that I robbed them at knife point. This was utterly ridiculous and ludicrous. They did not think so and arrested me for armed robbery.

CHAPTER ELEVEN

TRANSFORMING

Although I had been in the custody of LAPD before, somehow I felt this was a bit more serious than previously. I had not robbed anyone and I knew eventually I would be exonerated, but I also knew that this could be a lengthy process. All I could think about was the fact I had only paid two weeks in rent.

Once again I found myself at the Main County jail awaiting transfer to Wayside Ranch. It was going to take at least two weeks in order to get a court appearance. A couple of days before my court date, an investigator from the public defender's office came and interviewed me in the attorney's room. He was very debonair, yet reserved and was so programmed that I could sense he had done this many times before. Accordingly he told me that a public defender would be coming in and speaking with me after our conversation.

Basically he wanted my version of what happened so I proceeded to explain that I had been walking to the Mexican food truck just as I have done on many occasions. I told him that I only had two dollars and twenty-five cents in my possession and had asked two ladies in passing for change. He inquired what was their response. I told him that they did not respond. He wanted to know whether I thought that to be unusual and I didn't, considering the area that we were in, there are many Latinos who do not speak or understand English, he agreed. I added that the police had stopped me before I could make it to the truck.

Unlike other investigators I had come into contact with over the years, this one seemed to believe me, which brought an inkling of relief to this distressing situation. He instructed me to wait in the other room until the public defender came in and spoke with me.

When she entered the room I noticed that she was a very attractive, petite, astute looking lady of Jewish decent probably in her mid-forties. She articulately introduced herself as Peg, then explained the charges that I was facing and the potential punishment which, if convicted, included a substantial prison commitment. She said the Probation Report proved favorable, citing that I had successfully completed probation in the past. My record reflected no prior criminal convictions and was virtually spotless. She noticed that I was a full-time student at CSULA and said that this sort of record usually pleases most courts. She informed me that I would be going to court for a pre-trial hearing in about a week. Apparently my accusers would have to come and identify me as the culprit in order for the state to pursue any case against me. She made a soothing statement on her way out when she said that she believed my story. I asked her why and she said that she had been a public defender for many years and she just had a positive feeling. I thanked her and we agreed to see each other in court.

While awaiting my turn inside the holding tank at the Criminal Courts Building in downtown Los Angeles, I was extremely nervous because I did not know what to expect. I knew both the Investigator and Peg had said that they believed I was innocent, however I really did not believe them. I assumed this cynicism was the result of listening to all those "jail house lawyers." Nonetheless I was scared. All of a sudden Peg came in with this smile on her face, I immediately felt relieved. It seemed the two ladies who had accused me were known prostitutes. She said that no legal mind in the courtroom believed they would show up in the first place. She then went on to say this is a common accusation made by prostitutes, especially against black males, because the police are inclined to believe them. A robbery police report could be taken by the prostitute to her pimp for confirmation as to what happened to their money. In actuality their money was probably spent on drugs. Moses taught us if we want true deliverance, "Do not spread false reports. Do not help a wicked man by being a malicious witness" (Exodus 23:1). She told me the district attorney had agreed to drop the charges, which in her and my opinion, would be the right thing to do.

I mentioned to Peg, after the Judge dismissed the charges and ordered my immediate release, that it was easy for a black man to be wrongfully accused of a crime. She agreed and said fortunately there are some happy endings. However she admitted that too often there are not happy endings. I expressed gratitude to her for the vote of innocence and vowed to see her again one day. She said that would be nice; however hopefully it would be under very different circumstances and I agreed. We smiled and parted rather gracefully.

After I was released I hastily caught the bus back to my room. Since I had been gone for over two weeks I was anticipating that my possessions would have been confiscated. When I stuck my key inside the lock the door did not open. It was about 3:00 A.M. and my landlord lived clear across town in Compton. I called him and explained what had happened. He told me that he would be over in the morning and that I would just have to find some place to stay for the night. There I was on the streets of Los Angeles again, so I went and sat inside of a twenty-four hour donut shop with some other homeless people.

When my landlord arrived at dawn he was not pleased with my situation. I did not have a job or money. He graciously agreed to allow me a couple of weeks to find another place. When he opened the door to my room, surprisingly I noticed all my belongings were just as I had left them. In my prayers that night I asked God for direction.

When I spoke to Tania and explained my situation, her sensitive mother Emma Jean offered to allow me to stay in an apartment on the east side at no expense. Her goodwill gesture would afford me an opportunity to not only have a place to live, but also provide me the time to save up some money. However I was unfamiliar with Watts and felt that there had to be another way, I just needed to find it.

If my situation became critical I could go to Mae's house

but I knew that option would give her the satisfaction of seeing me in a position in need. My pride did not allow me to do that. I remember talking and praying intensely with my confidant Sunshine about my latest dilemma. Another friend Cliff had moved to the west side, an area of Los Angeles that I was more comfortable in, and offered to allow me refuge if I needed it.

After working hard a couple of months for Lav in the Testing Center and saving a couple of Welfare checks I moved into the Normandie Hotel located in the Wilshire District. This was somewhat of a retirement home. The proprietor said that she was a devout Christian and could feel that I was in need. A heavy burden had been lifted off of my shoulders. My room at that hotel was perfect for me. The entire hotel was quiet. As I was living there I was spending more time on campus and was working with several temporary agencies. Indeed, direction had been sacredly restored yet one more time.

One day while Yolanda and I were having lunch, she told me that she had been living with her boyfriend, who was about 12 years younger than her, and his mother. Since they all were not getting along, her boyfriend was forced to make a decision. It seemed that because the exterminators were fumigating their apartment, they had to find another place to stay for a few days. Yolanda was distraught because she could not understand why her boyfriend chose to make sure that his mother had a place to stay and not her. I was sympathetic to her concerns and remembered her reaction after I had chosen Feli over her during the recuperative stage of my illness. In an attempt to make retribution I tried to console her by offering my room as a place for her to stay. She came and stayed with me for a couple of days and I was happy that I could help her.

One day, while watching the Clarence Thomas Supreme

Court Confirmation Hearings on television, I heard crying outside of my window. When I investigated I saw about three large LAPD officers violently stumping this small man in the head. I did not see what had transpired before. However judging by the way he was being beaten, I suspect that he must have killed someone. There were many passing pedestrians and I remember seeing one of the officers looking up at my window as I yelled "Stop the brutality!" I quickly moved out of view because I did not want to be too conspicuous.

There was this stripper named "Susie" who danced at the club around the corner from the Normandie Hotel. She and I established a congenial relationship, full of compassion and understanding. She came to my room on some nights when she wanted to get away from it all. She had two kids that were living with their grandmother, but she could not stay there because her mother did not approve of her profession. She was a nice young Italian lady who made a lot of money "Strip Teasing." She offered me compensation on several occasions for letting her stay with me from time to time. But because I knew of her desire to get her children and herself into their own place, I did not allow her to give me any money.

One Sunday she and I got up early and went to the Faith Dome in South Central Los Angeles to hear the Word of God from Fredrick K.C. Price. She turned her life over to God that day and shortly afterwards got a job as a clerk. Eventually she got an apartment for her and her kids. Because I moved around so much, we have lost contact over the years; however her tenacious spirit has definitely left a reverberating effect on me.

My mother called me one day to tell me that my sister was coming to Los Angeles for a vacation. I felt indifferent about this because I had not in my heart forgiven them for the pain they had caused me in the past. When Cynthia came by my room, and we went further into our impromptu conversation, I felt as if she too was spying on me, reminiscent of the feelings I had when my brother had visited me in Seaside some years earlier. She and her friend Marylyn would be in LA for a week and she was hoping we could spend some time together. Reluctantly I agreed because I knew that the inner city of Los Angeles was not safe for two single ladies who did not know their way around.

The day that my sister was to leave, my landlord called me on the phone to offer an ultimatum—either I give her some money or I move out. When Cynthia came to say good-bye, I was rushing to get into the streets because I knew that as long as I stayed in that room I was not going to come up with the necessary money to pay rent. As Cynthia left my room that morning I remember she had this puzzled look on her face.

Cynthia had told me that my cousin Darnell was getting married in New Jersey and wanted me to be in his wedding. He called me and asked whether I would fly there. I explained to him my money situation, but still I assured him that I would make a gallant effort.

My openly gay friend on campus, Jesse, was a shrewd businessperson who had extensive contacts in the Airline Industry. He said that he could secure for me a round- trip ticket to Newark for $150. The only provision that he demanded was I not inquire how he was getting these inexpensive tickets. I told him to come by one night so we could make the transaction.

Before Jesse arrived I had gone out and had a few drinks, I remember sitting in the front seat of a "low rider" with two

Chloes sitting in the back. We were situated right smack in the middle of a "crack" cocaine-infested area. One of them pulled out a small bicycle chain, wrapped it around my neck and began to choke me, almost until I lost consciousness. Suddenly in the midst of my anguish all I could think about was the time when those LA County Sheriffs had administered the "choke hold" on me. I knew they wanted the ten dollars I was about to spend on the cocaine. However, I had again made a bad judgment and I had over three hundred dollars in my pocket; the alcohol had made me forget to take it out.

I was robbed and when I arrived back in the lobby of my hotel I saw Jesse there waiting for me. He could see something was wrong and I told him what had happened. However he refused to give me the ticket on credit because he said there were people with cash willing to buy. There I was sitting in my room, I had just lost my life's savings, not even thinking that I could have lost my life, and the phone rang and something was telling me that it was Darnell on the other end. Psalm 119:71 tells us, "It was good for me to be afflicted so that I might learn your decrees." Sure enough it was Darnell, and after telling him what had happened I could hear disappointment in his voice even though he insisted that he understood. I cried like a baby that night and once again it was so evident that I indeed had a problem. However, once again my pride did not allow me to admit it to even myself.

Kev was returning to the Virgin Islands, this time permanently, and I was again loosing a trusted confidant. I also was being evicted from the Normandie Hotel and suddenly I found myself homeless again. I remember thinking that if I could just make it to the next quarter of school I could get a big check and move back into the dorms. This was vital to my existence and would be the only way. After many cold sleepless nights and many days eating food that I was stealing out of the cafeteria, out of desperation I finally put my pride aside momentarily and moved back into the dorms. Surprisingly they assigned me to live in the exact same apartment that I had started my tenure in Los Angeles.

However this time all three of my roommates were African-American and were not athletes. It was unfortunate for me however that I would be sharing a room with a depressed, retired athlete. Roy was his name and I had some prior knowledge of him. Because of his infamous reputation I had formed some preconceived opinions about him. However I was not in the position to dictate what was occurring. So I learned rather quickly how to tolerate him.

My other two roommates were named Clint and Stevie. Both of them were bookworms and computer wizards. By then I had promised myself that I was going to concentrate more on my studies. I was getting closer to graduating and wanted to complete this task.

Roy, I found out rather quickly, had a severe drug and drinking problem. He also in my opinion was suffering from post-injury depression. He had apparently been a world-class sprinter who had torn a ligament in his knee and it was not healing as quickly as he wanted. His entire existence was dependent on that knee healing and on his track and field career, nothing else mattered to him with the exception of girls. His scholarship had been revoked after he did not recuperate quickly and the Athletic Department abandoned him. In many aspects his deep depression was warranted, without his scholarship he was an independent student just like the rest of us. The Old Testament prophet Jeremiah wrote, "So I say, 'My splendor is gone and all that I had hoped from the Lord'" (Lamentations 3:18). Roy had no job skills and was having a difficult time adjusting to his demoted splendor. He resorted to alcohol and drugs to help him cope with his depression.

I believe that I may have represented hope in Roy's eyes. He saw that I was sufficiently independent and, just like Johnny B and others, quickly proclaimed himself part of my family. I accepted this big brotherly role, yet Roy was unlike my other partners in that he had a legitimate dislike for education and wallowed in his own mud.

Stevie and Clint, on the other hand, represented what I had deep inside wanted to always be, a virtuous scholar. They were two of the most disciplined students I had come in contact with since Rhonda. They could go inside their room and study for literally hours. They were business majors too, and we saw each other a lot on campus. Stevie was a local student and went home often. Clint and Roy were just as I was, thousands of miles away from home. Clint was from Detroit and Roy was from East St. Louis. Also, like me, they had had traumatic experiences and were estranged from their respective families.

There was a benefit however in having Roy as my roommate—he was hardly home. He spent most of his time over at his girlfriend's apartment. He was dating this beautiful cultured Filipino girl named Maria. Roy loved her a lot and was extremely overly protective of her. There were many nights when he would come home mad after having an argument with someone about her.

I remember my buddy Rodney from Sacramento who was a star on the basketball team and was also an admirer of Maria's.

Often Roy would object to our friendship, he was paranoid and thought I was plotting with Rodney to take Maria away from him.

Becky had come back from maternity leave to work in the EOP. She was extremely elated to see that I was still on campus and greeted me with a legitimate hug. She immediately resumed responsibility as my counselor. I asked why she was doing this, she replied by saying that we had started something that she intended for us to finish. And just as my counselor had told me at Hartnell, she said that I was getting incredibly close to earning a Bachelor's degree in Business Administration. Becky had always been the motivating force behind my diligence. I am not sure how she knew, but I needed that drive and motivation that she was instinctively providing for me.

There was this young lady that worked in the EOP office that had become my friend rather quickly. She was a devout Christian and spoke of her faith in God often in my presence. Those of us who knew her best called her Boo. She and I grew in our relationship and soon became confidants. She was genuinely intrigued by my lifestyle and would ask about it and the places I had been in my life. She was concerned about my faith in God. She told me about her family and her boyfriend. She told me how much they loved each other. But still she asked me often how would I handle being involved with a person of a different faith. "My people come to you, as they usually do, and sit before you to listen to your words, but they do not put them into practice. With their mouths they express devotion, but their hearts are greedy for unjust gain" (Ezekiel 32:31). Apparently her boyfriend studied Islam. I knew who she was talking about since all of us lived in the dorms at that time. Although it seemed to me that they were so incompatible I felt that if Boo was happy, I was happy for her.

In apartment 217 one night Roy had come home drunk. He had put something on the stove and fallen asleep. We all were awakened by the fire alarm. This was déjà vu—it recalled the time I had fallen asleep in Jacko's house and almost burned the entire condo down. Nonetheless I believe that this was the straw that broke the camel's back as far as Stevie and Clint were concerned. They both were contemplating moving and this decided the issue. Stevie said he was moving back home with his parents because he was getting married. And Clint wanted me to move into a two-person apartment on campus with him as my roommate. Because of the size of 217 we wanted to stay there. However Roy refused to move out and, since he had practically burned up the entire kitchen, both Clint and I agreed that we would move to another apartment on campus as soon as the quarter ended. Roy became even more distressed. It was not our intentions to leave him alone like that but his hysteria and depression had become unbearable. So when the quarter ended Clint and I moved to a ground floor apartment. The apartment was somewhat smaller than 217 but for the first time I had my own room.

My mother called me one morning in the summer of 1988 and told me that she and Herb were coming to Los Angeles for a vacation and that they wanted to come and visit me. I had mixed emotions concerning her intentions and sought the council of my closest friends. I was unsure whether I even wanted to see my mother. Yet whether I liked it or not, they were coming and they would be stopping by to see me. Luckily I had a class about the same time that they would be on campus so I would not have to spend the entire day with them. They did have an opportunity to meet a few people around campus while they were touring. They invited me to have dinner with them later that evening and I accepted. They were hoping to meet Feli, although I explained to them that she had left California some time ago and that I did not expect to ever see her again.

My mother and Herb left Los Angeles after a few days and I can honestly say that I was rather happy to see them go. I am not sure why I felt this way but I am sure that I really did not want to see my mother and Herb then. Maybe, it was because of what had happened between us several years earlier in Richmond. Or possibly, I was feeling somewhat rebellious because of the insurance policy incident from when I was in the hospital. I definitely had some ill feelings toward her and her companion.

There was a big story in the campus newspaper about a Ninja terrorizing female co-eds in the dorm. The culprit, apparently had been dressing up in Ninja clothing and was peeping in the female students' dorm windows late at night. With the assistance of the LAPD, the campus police vowed to apprehend the Ninja. Rumor had the Ninja as elusive and extremely familiar with the campus. There were even reports that he had actually entered the apartment of a female student through the window. The Ninja had become the subject of much dialogue in and out of the classrooms. Everyone knew the Ninja had to be a university student and we all were anxiously awaiting his capture.

Two weeks into the Summer quarter 1988 Roy knocked on my door and said that the Ninja had been captured. We went to Clint's room to tell him but he was not there. This was unusual for him because he was always at home during that time of the morning. Roy and I assumed that he had an early meeting on campus.

When we got on campus and read in the newspaper that it was Clint who they had apprehended, we were astonished. We thought it was a big mistake; however plain as day there his name was written, they even gave an account of his capture. Apparently he had been inside of a female student's room. The student must have awakened to find Clint dressed in a Ninja costume staring at her. Allegedly she screamed and in a flash the Ninja was out of the window. Her roommates called the campus police and they caught Clint in his car changing his clothes.

This surprised us because Clint was an extremely quiet individual who basically kept to himself. Those of us who knew him well also knew that he was somewhat interested in the Martial Arts. But we also knew Clint was a timid person, those of us who knew him best would never have thought he was capable of this. In our opinion he did not have the nerves. Roy and I went back to my apartment and searched his things, because we knew that eventually the investigators would be coming. While going through Clint's belongings we found several female disguises. It quickly became apparent that Clint indeed had an alter ego.

I was aware that he went out sometimes late at night, in fact, that by itself was not unusual because I had similar habits. What was peculiar was the fact that I had absolutely no knowledge that Clint cross-dressed on occasions. I assume that he did that in order to go places where men could not.

Since Roy had outstanding warrants for his arrest he could not go near the county jail to visit Clint. So I visited him, and he basically willed his entire belongings to me because he was unaware of his future and how long he was going to be incarcerated. I could very much sympathize with his dilemma and I tried to help as much as I could. As much trouble as I'd been in, I had never faced anything like this. The Los Angeles County District Attorney's intentions were to send him to state prison. However, the public defender felt that he might have a mental defect and was requesting a 90-day observation. Clint was indeed committed to state prison, but fortunately for him for only the 90-day observation. Habakkuk 3:2 tells us, "Lord, I have heard of your fame; I stand in awe of your deed, O lord. Renew them in our day, in our time make them known; in wrath remember mercy." I prayed that God would deliver him from what ever it was he was going through.

There was one bright spot in all this. I had the apartment all to myself for the entire summer. Roy was not hanging around as much because he had moved with Maria into an off-campus apartment. I accomplished more academically that quarter than I ever had and I made up my mind that I was going to succeed at almost any sacrifice.

When Fall Quarter came around Rodney wanted to be my roommate. I was somewhat skeptical about his proposal because of his status on campus, there would be more people around than I would prefer. However I also knew that he and Roy did not get along so I would not have that distraction to deal with. So I consented to being Rodney's roommate for that quarter.

That was my senior year and, since my classes were more intense, I had to become more focused. Larry was graduating and he had decided to leave California for his native city of Atlanta. He wanted me to go with him and even offered to facilitate the relocation. I had been reading and hearing of a large exodus to Atlanta by black professionals and I was quite intrigued by his suggestion. However my heart was in Los Angeles and I respectfully declined his invitation. Nonetheless this imminent closure to our relationship, for me, was a very sentimentally triumphant period in my life. Roy was still getting high. Ray was still struggling with the street life. June was on his way to prison. Cliff was writing movie scripts. In fact, I knew that I was experiencing a transcendence.

One fall 1988 evening I fell and hurt my back on my way up the stairs to my apartment. The doctor at the Health Center prescribed some painkillers. Trying to get high, I took a handful of them at once and chased them with a fifth of brandy. A friend stopped by and we smoked some crack. As I was withdrawing from all this, I fell into this deep depression. My entire life's journey was flashing before me. I begun to think about my life and all the negativity I had experienced. The direction out of my loneliness and depravity was irresoluble. Subconsciously, I must have been more depressed than I realized and wanted to reach out to my family and needed them to reach out to me. So I called my brother and sisters in an attempt to gain compassion. I don't know why, since we were not raised compassionately. Moses wrote, "If this is how you are going to treat me, put me to death right now-if I have found favor in your eyes-and do not let me face my own ruin" (Numbers 11:15). And despondently I told them that I was going to commit suicide. I apologized for the embarrassment I had brought them over the years. Junie and Cynthia seemed indifferent toward my intentions. However, during my conversation with Sandra, she insisted that I call my mother right away. Although I wanted to speak with my mother, I told Sandra I didn't. Shortly after hanging up the phone with her my mother called, but as always she really didn't have anything to say, no wisdom to impart, no advice to give, no solutions to render and definitely no compassion or Agape to share. This was normal for her because as far back as I can remember we had always had difficulties in communicating.

The next thing I remember the campus police were standing over me with their automatic revolvers pointed at my torso, they were yelling for me to slowly remove my hands from under the covers. I concurred as I saw Rodney standing there also with this huge smile on his face. The Assistant Director of Housing was there too.

Apparently my mother had called the LAPD from Richmond and they in turn got in touch with the campus police. Then they contacted the housing administrators who brought them to my room. I tried to explain that all this had been a big misunderstanding and that my mother had overreacted. I told them that I had no intentions of committing suicide, told them good evening and thanked them for their concern. They told me to put on some pants. The officers then told me that they were going to take me to the hospital to see if I had taken any type of drug that would be detrimental to my health. I informed them that was not necessary because I was fine. But still, they forcefully insisted and put me in handcuffs, bound my legs together, then threw me in their squad car.

They took me to a place I was very familiar with—the County/USC Medical Center. We stayed there for the entire day and they took blood samples from me. This made me nervous because I knew that I had used cocaine the previous night and thought it might still be in my system. Oddly it was not and the doctors told us that I showed minimal traces of alcohol. The officer took me back to campus. When I went to check my mailbox I saw Ralph, he informed me that Lorraine wanted to talk to me. He also called me into an office where he began to ask me what happened. I told him that I had been drinking and wanted to play a game with my family. I assured him that I was not contemplating committing suicide and that I never would. He looked at me as if to say he believed me, and said that there were a lot of people up on the main campus who wanted to see me.

After a couple of grueling days and about fifteen inquisitive minds, I finally got the message across that I was not crazy. Although I did not tell them the entire story, I knew exactly what had happened and said to myself that I would have to watch myself more closely. I was aware of the possibility of depression in the withdrawal stages of any drug. Until then I had been fortunate never to experience that state. As I was having a drink with Sunshine and telling him about this calamity, we laughed and began to search and examine Scripture trying to find some reasons for my recent mishap.

The holiday season was approaching and as always I was spending it with June and his family. His sister Renee brought her sexy friend named Karen over in the late evening. I left with them and we all went back to Renee's apartment. Apparently, Karen was waiting for a man friend to pick her up. I was waiting for a young lady to call me. After about three hours we came to the conclusion that we were both being stood up. Karen and I began to talk intensely once Renee had fallen asleep. Our conversation turned into intimacy, and the beginning of a loving relationship. We were together all the time. She would bring her two boys over to my apartment on the weekends. Karen knew most of my faults and wanted to help me with them, however unlike what I was accustomed to, she was a family oriented person and wanted to bear me a child. My friends would joke with me about one day soon moving out of the dorms with her. Considering the amount of time that we spent together the idea had seriously crossed my mind.

Karen unknowingly was competing for my affection with Tania. In fact, neither of them knew about the other. My fleshly desires were with Karen; however, she possessed an evil spirit that reminded me of Jean. She was still harboring dire emotions toward men, I believe, because of the way her estranged husband had treated her. Apparently, after ten years of marriage, he had left his family for another woman. This had a negative reverberating effect on her trust. Since she was not a very spiritual young lady, we were unequally yoked and our relationship was in essence doomed from the start.

Tania, on the other hand, would refrain from sexual relations which was also very different than what I was used to. She told me that she was saving herself for her husband and was adamant about that. She thought that I would make a good husband. However, Tania was a ritzy kid and was very educated and cultured. She was not going to allow herself to become seriously involved with a man who was not financially secure and spiritually sound. I respected her position because I knew what perpetual spiritual education could do to an individual. The apostle Paul told us to "Speak to one another with psalms, hymns and spiritual songs. Sing and make music in your heart to the Lord" (Ephesians 5:19). We were content with our relationship. We also knew the Holy Spirit was present whenever we were together.

In early December 1988 my mentor Ralph had gotten me an internship with a major computer company. I was an assistant to a prosperous salesman named Andre. He knew Ralph from their associations at First AME Church in South Central. Andre took it upon himself to teach me the vital aspects of his profession, although his specialty seemed to be motivational speaking and he always knew the appropriate dialogue to initiate. He told me often that I was gifted in certain areas and that I should ask God to reveal those areas to me. He had flourished in his profession and he needed to release his gifts in a divinely imposed manner. I was apt to listen to him because he possessed the same astute qualities as did Robert Griffin, and he had the confidence of Mel Mason.

Clint had been released from prison and had come over to stay with us for a couple of days. However Rodney was uncomfortable with having the ex-Ninja sleeping in our apartment. It really did not bother me because I knew that Clint was harmless. Rodney did not know him the way I did and out of respect for him I had to ask Clint to find another place to stay. I bought some of Clint's belongings because he was desperate for money. I did not want him to go and do something rash.

One morning Roy and another one of our friends were knocking real hard on my door. Karen and I had been up all night passionately making love so I was reluctant to even answer the door. However their persistence dictated my actions and I eventually answered it. By the distressed look on their faces I could tell something was wrong. They told me that the LAPD had found Clint dead in his car. He had apparently committed suicide by hooking the exhaust up to the inside of the car. This was an atrocity. All I could think of was this troubled individual and how his life had disintegrated at a rapid pace. Solomon wrote to us in the latter stages of his life, "Again I looked and saw all the oppression that was taking place under the sun: I saw the tears of the oppressed-and they have no comforter; power was on the side of their oppressors and they have no comforter" (Ecclesiastes 4:1). His parents flew out from Detroit and took his body back there for burial. They had not seen him in over thirteen years.

I was depressed for quite some time because of this. Once again I went on a drinking binge, trying to figure out whether there was something I could have done to prevent this. One night, while still on this binge, I went over to a friend's apartment and borrowed her car. She had lent me her car on several occasions to go and purchase drugs. She was an occasional user of "crack" so, sensing my destination, she basically just told me to hurry back.

On my way to MacArthur Park to "score" I was stopped on the freeway by the Highway Patrol and I was ordered to pull the car over into this vacant gas station in downtown Los Angeles. After failing a field sobriety test I was arrested for driving under the influence. I knew that I had not flunked that test and I insisted that they administer a breathalyzer test. But, when we got to Parker Center they did not give me a test and I was booked and thrown in a cell to await transfer to Los Angeles County Jail.

This time I knew that I would be there for a while. The public defender said since this was my third offense I should just wait it out to see what kind of deal the district attorney might offer. She said that I would be incarcerated for at least three months. My only concern was my personal belongings at

CSULA. I knew that if someone did not go to get them that I would probably lose everything. So I called Renee and Karen to ask them to go pick up my things, they said that they would. I assumed that they immediately went to do what I had requested, however I found out later they never did.

Every two weeks I had to make another appearance in the courts. Each time I was transferred to a different jail facility, I managed to run into both June and his brother Joe. Joe Lee had been committed to serve a small amount of jail time for joy riding. However, June's fate was state prison for drug related convictions.

Pinky, my friend, whose car that I was driving at the time of my arrest, had been stripped in that vacant lot. Fred told me this during one of our phone conversations. At my request Pinky came to visit me at the Biscaluz Center and I told her what had happened. I asked her to forgive me, and I offered to help her to get another car when I got out. She told me that she knew my mishaps were not intentional.

About three days later I was summoned to the interviewing room, apparently there were two investigators who wanted to speak with me. They told me they had some questions to ask me concerning Pinky's car. They asked me whether she and I had been intimate. I told them we had on occasions. They then asked me how many times, I told them about seven or eight, then they looked at each other and smiled. One said to the other, "You see, I told you so." I asked them what was it that they were trying to find out. They said that the young lady had accused me of stealing her car. However after they talked with her they were somewhat skeptical of her accusations. They said that I had enough problems to deal with. They went on to say that they felt that the young lady was somewhat bitter because of the condition that she had found the car in. They said that they believed my story and unless some other evidence surfaced to discredit my statement I would not hear from them again. Luckily for me I never did.

Karen came to see me twice; she had adamantly declared, in the past, that she would never come to a jail to see anyone. However she came to see me and made me feel special. I was not mad when I found out that they did not go and get my stuff. I had begun to write these things off. However I trusted Rodney and thought he would take care of my personal belongings.

One day I called Roger, the Director of Housing, and informed him of my condition. He said that he would take care of everything. He said that he would put all of my things in storage. I thanked him. He asked me whether I had called Becky and informed her of my whereabouts. When I spoke with Becky she was very much displeased with my predicament. And she was legitimately concerned about when I would be returning. I did not know and she asked me the same questions that Roger had, which was why I had not called her sooner. I told her that I was hoping that I would be released sooner and they would not have had to find out about this unfortunate situation that I was in. She said that she would withdraw me from classes because of hardship, I thanked her.

After about a week or so I mustered enough pride to call Tania. She, just like Roger and Becky, was somewhat distraught over the fact that I had not called her sooner. She wanted me to call her when I got out so that she could offer me a place to stay for a few days. She had just gotten an apartment and it was small, but she still agreed to allow me refuge until I found a more permanent arrangement, I thanked her. When I got off of the phone I felt a renewed affection for Tania. It was unlike any feeling that I had had before—towards anyone. I could not understand why I had not contacted her sooner. Tania would have gone to that apartment and gotten my things. She had offered before to give me a place on the east side. It was Tania's family that had embraced me. It was me, who because of my pride could not discern this revelation. Sometimes we search so hard for things we need and all the time those desired necessities are right under our noses.

Finally, after 90 days of incarceration I made it to Division 100 which is the final stop for an inmate in the judiciary process within Los Angeles County, this division would determine my fate. The public defender came in and told me that the Judge did not want to send me to state prison. But she also told me the district attorney did. She informed me that if I would plea guilty to reckless driving under the influence, the Judge would sentence me to time served and I would be released that night. This was indeed a pleasure to my ears so I pleaded guilty and was released that night. I had escaped state prison once again.

After I was freed I went to Tania's house and stayed with her for a week. She was studying for the CPA exam and I knew the importance of this test and I did not want to impose on her much longer. So I went to Renee's house and offered her some money and she agreed to allow me to stay with her for a while. This also presented an opportunity for Karen and me to spend more time together. However, during the entire time that I was living at Renee's, I was going back and forth to Tania's.

Karen and I went to CSULA's campus to survey the remains of my things. Rodney had moved out of the dorms and I knew this would not be a good sign because he was from Sacramento. If he had stolen my things I probably would never get them back. When the maintenance guy took us to the storage room where they were keeping my things I noticed that there did not seem to be a lot there. I noticed that most of my clothes were missing and some of my electronics were gone. My computer, two of my televisions and my VCR were all missing. Both Karen and I felt this loss, for the first time she understood why I felt so strongly about her going to get my things. All I knew was that I would have to start over once again.

Karen had begun to lash out at me because she was still suffering from the residual effects of her failed marriage. I was aware of her inner pain and took a lot of verbal abuse from her. Although I could understand what she was going through considering her troubled past, I just wished that she would have talked with me more about it, as opposed to thinking that her advocate was her adversary. I could sense that our relationship was coming to an end, if not for her, for me, because I had begun to spend more time with the Spirit-filled Tania and Pam. And those vibrant young, yet seasoned cultured women had experienced much Providence in their lives. It was evident to me that I was changing, I wanted more of what they possessed.

However I was not sure if it was the education or my past experiences that were changing my thought patterns. "This is what we speak, not in words taught us by human wisdom, but in words taught by the Spirit, expressing spiritual truths in spiritual words. The man without the Spirit does not accept the things that come from the Spirit of God, for they are foolishness to him, and he cannot understand them, because they are spiritually discerned" (1 Corinthians 2:13-14). All I knew was that I kept hearing this Voice in my head telling me that my life was about to profoundly and divinely change.

CHAPTER TWELVE

POINT BLANK

Eventually Renee wanted her space back and asked me to move out. I anticipated this and had gotten Cliff's approval for my occasional sleepover. Although I frequently slept on his floor I still considered myself homeless because often I found myself sleeping in classrooms. There were nights when I was forced to sleep in the bleachers of the stadium on campus. But I wasn't the only one, there were other students who slept in classrooms and the locker rooms. Each of us seemed to know the best places to "crash." I had secured my clothes in a locker at the gym where I also kept a portable iron. I took my showers, ate and sought solitude during the late night hours, free not only from charge but also the cold of the outdoors.

After a month of homelessness just as I had anticipated Karen and I agreed to go our separate ways. Yet I believed that it was not what either of us wanted then. I felt that she needed the satisfaction of knowing that she had left someone just as her husband had left her. In my case I had always felt that I was just an emotional rebound she was experiencing for her self-esteem after her failed marriage. And, I really did not want to continue to put myself through that.

At the end of Winter Quarter 1989, one day, while chatting with Sunshine, he showed me this ad in the campus newspaper. Apparently this engineering professor was looking for a live-in student to care for his elderly mother. The ad stated that the arrangement included free rent and salary in exchange for the help in caring for his mother. Sunshine suggested that I answer the ad, and since by then I had been homeless for several weeks, I did.

Professor Barnett was an instructor in the engineering department with full tenure who had been teaching at CSULA for over twenty years. He was in his mid-sixties and said that his mother was ninety-five years old. He was looking for a male student who could live with his mother at her condo in Alhambra. The student would have to stay with her during the daytime hours. He said there was a Chinese couple who were exchange students that he had hired to care for his mother during the evening hours. He went on to inform me that he did not live with his mother and he had another house a little closer to campus. After that he offered me the job and an additional four hundred dollars a month salary.

This astonished me because these were advent people. Curiosity mandated that I ask the professor why would he trust me around his ninety-five year old bourgeoisie mother. He told me that he had interviewed several people from many different races and backgrounds and I was the lone applicant who had impressed him after the initial conversation. He told me that I had this trustworthiness about myself and if his mother felt the same way I could move in at once.

I went by Mom Barnett's condo that afternoon and was pleasantly surprised to see how coherent she was, and found out later that she had had a career as an English teacher. She was a native New Yorker who still spoke with a very proper northeastern accent. I assumed she would be incoherent, considering her age. However the only notable illness she was experiencing was osteoporosis and was confined to a wheelchair. Accordingly this was the reason that Professor Barnett wanted a male student, someone who could lift her in and out of the bed and toilet, and that basically was my job description during the day. Tao and Gee, the Chinese couple, had the same responsibilities during the evening while I attended classes. Mom Barnett gave her nod of approval and all of us moved in that night. This arrangement represented the best living conditions I had experienced since my days in Jacko's condo in Monterey. There was a swimming pool outside of the front door and I was surprised at how the neighbors reacted to me, they all seemed to be very polite people. Everything was working just as the professor had said that it would.

Both Tao and Gee were in their late forties. Although there were many Asian students in my business classes I had never lived with any. I assumed that I had some stereotypical views toward them and visa versa. But I soon discovered that those stereotypical views were unwarranted because those were two of the most genuine people that I had ever encountered. They immediately started to call me their son because they did not have any children yet. I could sense that maybe there were some ulterior motives for their attitudes towards me but it did not bother me. Tao, in her innate wisdom, had this ability to sense when I needed to talk. Jesus Christ taught, "All that belongs to the father is mine. This is why the Spirit will take from what is mine and make it known to you" (John 16:15). When Tao came to this country as an exchange student a couple of years earlier, she had accepted the Christian faith. She was studying organic chemistry at CSULA and she already had a Doctorate in that field from China, but in America that did not mean anything because American companies would not honor it so she had to start all over again. She was a very beautiful person who had a great personality. Even though she spoke very little English she was gifted, in that she could communicate with her expressions and demeanor. Her number one priority wasn't to get an American degree but to become an American citizen and she conducted herself accordingly. Her responsibilities at Mom Barnett's included keeping the condo clean and occasionally cooking on the weekends.

Gee, her husband, was a compulsive swimmer and was very much in love with his Chinese culture, as he should have been. He refused to relinquish it to the mainstream American way of life and he was very much different from Tao in that way. Gee was fascinated with the American dollar, and his primary concern and driving force was to get as many of them as quickly as possible. While Tao sought knowledge, Gee pursued money. He was a legal hustler and reminded me of my father in some ways because of his love of his native country. Gee was a delightful person to be around because he had a great sense of humor. He did for Mom Barnett during the evening what I was doing for her in the morning.

Tao and Gee both would always mention a venture they wanted to include me in, but they said that they did not want to describe it until they were ready. Not only did they look after mom but they also concerned themselves with my welfare as well.

I was getting real close to graduating and had begun to spend even more of my time in the library. Late one spring night I was riding a bike home when some white Alhambra police officers stopped me and ordered me off of my bike and face down on the ground. They addressed me in very explicit, racial terms. They asked me what was I doing in that neighborhood during that hour of night. I told them that I was on my way home from the library at CSULA. They answered sarcastically and took me into the station. Their reason for taking me into the station was that I fit the description of a purse snatcher. This was something I had heard before. It was obvious where I was coming from considering the large amount of books that I was carrying.

The Alhambra police department detained me for two days, and the entire time that I was in custody the only thing on my mind was my responsibilities at Mom Barnett's house. But, I had gotten to use the telephone and had called Professor Barnett to tell him that there were a couple of things that I had to take care of and that I was unsure when I would return. He told me that he would get one of his other students to watch Mom Barnett while I was away. He did not ask me any questions but I could tell from the tone in his voice that he was disappointed. He had warned me against being out late at night in that area. He told me in advance that I might be mistaken for a burglar because of the racial make-up in that community. Eventually, the police released me, saying the individual who had reported the purse being stolen did not identify me as being the culprit.

One day, while I was taking care of Mom Barnett, a well-dressed Hispanic male about my age entered the door. We always kept the front door unlocked. He identified himself as "Lotto." We had heard a lot about him from the Barnetts. Apparently Lotto had taken care of Mom Barnett for several years before we moved in. He and I had many things in common, he was an extremely well-mannered person. He was a student at CSULA who did not live too far from us. He was employed at a law firm in Hollywood. He liked to party all of the time and spent a large amount of his free time in nightclubs all over Los Angeles.

The Barnetts treated Lotto like a son, but because he had recently moved in with his girlfriend I could sense some animosity between him and Professor Barnett. I believe this to be the case because Professor Barnett had brought Lotto to the United States from Mexico when he was just a child, specifically to care for Mom Barnett. In fact, it appeared that Professor Barnett was jealous of all of Lotto's interpersonal relationships.

Roy once again began to spend a lot of time around me. He would come over to Mom Barnett's condo quite often because of an infatuation that he had developed for Tao. He seemed indifferent to the fact that Tao was married and a lot older than us. Roy and I would hang out over at Lotto's a lot, mostly because of the cocaine habit that he had. I remember that his girlfriend told him often that she was going out with her girlfriends when we would come over. This was a little strange to me because everyday she was going out with her girlfriends. However Lotto refused to believe that anything was unusual. He thought that she was making excuses for not wanting to be around us while we were doing drugs. This could have been the case because Roy's girlfriend was the same way.

Early one morning, while hung over and late for class, I received a phone call from Renee whom I had not heard from in a while. She informed me that my partner Champ had just arrived in Los Angeles from Denver and was at the Greyhound bus station in downtown Los Angeles. She gave me a phone number where I could reach him. Although I had not seen Champ since my early days in Seaside, I had received postcards from him from all over the country. Champ and I had always been good friends.

When he answered the phone I could tell that he was in need from the sound of his voice. After asking what it was that I could do for him, he said that he had just gotten off of the bus and was short of money and that he needed a place to stay. Since my room was big enough for him to make a pallet on the floor, and since I was compelled to help him for some reason, I went to pick him up.

Roy, Champ and Lotto all became very good friends rather quickly, which was advantageous for me because my priorities had become my classes. I was unbelievably very close to completing my degree and did not need or want any undesired distractions. Champ was familiar with Los Angeles and knew his way around. He had a son and an ex-wife who lived in Long Beach and would go and stay with them for days at a time, affording me the privacy that I needed.

Champ was no longer addicted to weed as he was when we were living in Monterey. He was now using heroin. However his use of it was discreet and he managed to keep it away from me. When I confronted him about it, he did not deny it. 2 Peter 1:15 tells us, "And I will make every effort to see that after my departure you will always be able to remember these things." The Lord was showing me something by Champ's actions. Champ would leave for days at a time because he knew that there was a line that I would not cross with him.

One day his parents were visiting Los Angeles on a vacation. They had spoiled their only son Champ and loved him with all of their heart and soul. Because they did not know how to find him they came by the condo to see me. Champ's parents and I had managed to maintain a cordial relationship over the years ever since our MPC days and I welcomed their visit. Yet when they came to see me I did not know where Champ was but I could discern from the look on their faces that they were worried that they might not get an opportunity to see their son while they were in Los Angeles. But since they were going to be in town for a couple of weeks I knew that this would give me some time to at least try to track him down. After they told me where they were staying, I set out on a mission to find Champ in the vast metropolis of Los Angeles.

By faith Champ called me that same afternoon, and as expected he did not know that his parents were in town. After he told me where he was I went to get him and took him to see his parents. Apparently by choice he had been staying in a hotel on skid row. He could have gotten a job and lived anywhere he wanted to but I had never known Champ to work a day in his life. Whenever he needed money he would just pick up the telephone, and no matter where in this world he was his parents would just send it to him.

While his parents and I were visiting I could not in good conscience tell them, as Champ and I had previously discussed, that he was in dire need of money. I was torn between loyalty to my friend and being honest to his aging parents. Should I tell them about Champ's drug addiction that would probably kill him? Or, should I remain quiet, letting them continue to support his habit? I honestly did not know what to do, so I just let it go because of the friendship that Champ and I shared, which was undoubtedly deeper than the concern that I may have held for those people.

Champ's parents left Los Angeles and as usual they left him with a large sum of money. And, as usual, Champ disappeared into the vastness of southern California. But this time it didn't bother me that much, even though I knew that I probably wouldn't be seeing my good friend for a while.

In early June 1989, one warm evening, while in my room studying for my upcoming final examinations, I heard a commotion out in the hallway. Mom Barnett had not been feeling well and Professor Barnett had been spending more time than usual at her house. As I went to see what was going on, I noticed Tao, Gee and the professor standing in Mom Barnett's room. When I went inside her room and looked at her I could tell that something was wrong, very wrong. She was having trouble sitting up in bed and appeared to be having trouble breathing. So I attempted to assist them in getting her up. But suddenly I heard this groaning sound, which apparently was Mom Barnett's last breath. As I was holding her in my arms, I could not only see, but also feel death come over her. Her face went pale. Her body grew cold. Many thoughts flashed quickly through my mind as I witnessed life turn into death. So close but yet so far away.

Mom Barnett reminded me of that soldier who lay dead after that overdose. I knew at that moment how my mother and Junie must have felt when they helplessly watched my father pass on into glory. If that experience was anything such as I was experiencing then, what a helpless feeling that must have been. Selfishly, once again all I could hear was that Voice telling me that my life would be different.

The Barnetts did not have a lot of family and the professor quickly decided to have Mom Barnett's remains cremated and scattered in the Pacific Ocean. I knew he loved that old woman with every inch of his existence so when she died we all knew it would be very hard on him and it was. But it was also hard on Lotto, he was never the same after Mom Barnett's death. Mom Barnett had been the only mother that he had ever known. Since Lotto was still suffering from a now failed relationship with his girlfriend, with help from Tao and Gee I found myself acting as the healer.

When the closure process had been completed Professor Barnett sat down with us and discussed his plans for the condo. He was going to clear out the condo and settle it with the owners of the property. Yet he was generous and allowed us to remain there for two months rent free. This was extremely laudable of him because by the end of that period I would have graduated from CSULA and hopefully have a job. Although we all discussed the possibility of keeping the condo I don't believe that any of us had the money to do that. Tao and Gee did have other ventures in mind and wanted to experience life in America from a different perspective. But before they left they discussed with me what they had been telling me all those months they wanted to discuss.

Tao and Gee were soon joined in Los Angeles by their

number two daughter, Shi Tao. They told me how their number one daughter Ben Young could not seem to acquire a visa to leave communist China. Apparently the only way that Ben Young could get out of mainland China was if she married an American citizen. They went on to say that they considered me as their son and how wonderful it would be if I were to travel to Shanghi and marry Ben Young. They insisted that she and I establish immediate dialogue which we did. I had heard about these sorts of arrangements and I was made aware that it was legal as long as we remained married for a period of time. They told me that Ben Young was an engineer, and that there was a Chinese engineering firm here in the states that was interested in hiring her. Their proposal intrigued me because after seeing a picture of Ben Young and receiving a letter from her, I felt as if I had known her all of my life. After mixed opinions from my friends, I agreed to go to China to marry and bring back Ben Young.

Early one Saturday June 1989 morning I participated in the commencement services at California State University at Los Angeles. I was graduating with a Bachelor's of Science degree in Business Administration, Administrative Management. Most of my buddies were there to cheer me across the stage. Luke, the beloved physician, wrote in Acts 28:10, "They honored us in many ways and when we were ready to sail, they furnished us with the supplies we needed." My mentors were there, looking gratified. Tao and Gee were there. I remember the proud and joyful expression on Becky's face. I knew that my degree was hers as much as it was mine. There were mixed feelings I had about that day. I could not help but to think of all of my buddies that had started this journey with me but did not finish it. I sentimentally thought of those who had made it and had gone on in other directions. I thought about Robert, Mel, Bonnie and

Ignasio who were all there from the beginning when I was not sure of anything. I thought about Margarita and Feli, both of whom I wish could have been there. I thought about Rhonda who I knew would have been there had she known and who had told me years earlier that I could do it. I thought about Raymond whom had went through most of this with me. I thought about my family who I knew would not believe me until I showed them my diploma. I thought about my late father's words "One day your life will be different." That entire day I was the happiest man in the world.

Emma Jean, Tonia's mother offered me a job. In fact, there were people making all kinds of offers. There was also a viable option, graduate school, which I really did not want to attend at that point in my life. I was feeling relieved just to have earned a bachelor's degree. Dr. Bagot who was the only African-American full time instructor in the Business Department invited me to come in and speak with him about my plans for the future. He had in the past spoken with me on several occasions about starting a Black Business Student Association. However I was apprehensive about his request because I knew that apathy existed there on campus—especially amongst the black student population. Because of the grades that black students in business majors were receiving, compared to the grades that other students from different races were receiving, I could understand their lethargy. Quite frankly, we did not have faith in the system and subconsciously the black students in the business department had developed a "me, me" attitudes. Accordingly, I was one of two black males graduating with a business degree, in a graduating class of over seven hundred students.

The time rapidly approached when I had to move out of

the condo. I had saved some money and was prepared. I knew that if push came to shove I could go and stay with Cliff or Renee for a while. However, Champ had started to once again hang out around me and I was aware that I would have to make provisions for him also. Taking his homelessness into consideration, I needed to have a spot where he could lay his head from time to time. Eventually I settled on a two-bedroom small apartment in the Highland Park section of Los Angeles.

Roy, even though he was still living with Maria, had started dating this Chinese woman named Mary. About one week after graduating he and I were in her car en route to score crack in a section of East Los Angeles that was notorious for Mexican gangs, we were surrounded by twenty or more young Hispanic males and females demanding that we give them our money. After we refused, of course, one of them stuck a semi-automatic rifle, which resembled an "Uzi," inside of my window. Roy and I were so high on cocaine this did not faze us. Since Roy was driving, the "Chloe" was aiming the barrel right at his head. All of a sudden, on my signal, Roy hit the clutch and as we sped off we could hear these successive popping noises. Undoubtedly we were getting "dumped on."

Fortunately we were in motion, headed downhill, before the assailant could get a decent aim, allowing us to make it to yet another drug spot to cop. The next morning Roy came by to show me where one of the bullets had penetrated the vehicle. Apparently it was encased so close to where my back had been that we both knew that it was the grace of God that I was not paralyzed.

Eventually I found myself homeless but this time I ended up sleeping in an abandoned car in Roy's stall for about six months. Everything that I ate came from campus. There were people who wanted to help me but my pride got in the way. A friend on campus had promised me employment as soon as the budget permitted.

Tania had gotten married so my contact with her and her family had faded. By then Pam and I had become spiritually in tune with each other, but she was anxiously awaiting an acceptance letter from a medical school back East so I prepared myself to lose her too as a confidant. One day I stopped by Lotto's office since I had not seen or heard anything from him in a while. But when I asked the receptionist for him she had this peculiar expression on her face. Then she responded by saying "He is no longer with us." So I inquired whether she knew where I could find him. Then, she said "You don't understand." She went on to inform me that Lotto had been murdered in the MacArthur Park section of Los Angeles. After she told me where it happened and how he was killed I knew that it was drug related. Later I called Professor Barnett and he told me that Lotto had been staying with a prostitute in that area for a while, and ultimately he was shot point blank in the stomach by an unknown assailant.

Lotto's untimely demise left me numb. It left all of us who were close to him numb. Even though two months had passed since his death, I felt a sense of loss and abandonment. The last time that I saw him he was standing on a corner in the MacArthur Park section, smoking crack. Yet I did not think anything was wrong, I felt that he was just going through one of those binges that were so prevalent with all of us then. "We are aliens and strangers in your sight, as were all our forefathers. Our days on earth are like a shadow, without hope" (Chronicles 29:15). For the first time in my life I realized that our time here on earth is not promised to us and we can leave this place at any moment.

Lotto's demise, along with Roy's and my close brush with death, really shed some light on my own mortality. I know that those two instances were the beginning of a new era in my life, and marked the end of yet another epoch in my brief but perplexed life. I began to spend more time around Tao, Gee and Shi Tao because I was yearning more for the family life. Thinking that the family life would deliver me out of the pig troupe mentality that had imprisoned me for so many years, I also hung around June's family more. They had always treated me as if I was part of their family and were great therapy for my loneliness.

June had been sent back to prison so his younger brother Joe and I had become closer. Sometimes he would sneak me into the house late at night when Mae was asleep since he knew that I was homeless. After close to a year of homelessness, one night, when he wasn't at home, I was standing on the corner waiting to spot him in the sea of crack smokers when all of a sudden a car pulled up from behind me. Two Chloes exited the car, approached me, and stuck a sawed-off shotgun to the back of my head. I remember hearing the trigger being cocked. They called me by a familiar name although it was not mine. Divinely someone was standing there who knew the person they were looking for and told them that I was not the one. Just that fast, once again, my own mortality flashed before my eyes. I was reminded yet one more time that there was a Divine purpose for me and began to pay more and more attention to my surroundings.

After leaving Professor Barnett's Tao, Gee and Shi Tao had moved to El Monte which was not far from CSULA. They were working as live-in managers at this motel. We all had begun to make serious preparations for my voyage to China. Since I had been homeless for some time I was desperate to make that trip. This could not come at a more opportune time because I was tired of sleeping in Roy's car. I was tired of taking showers in the gym. And I was tired of riding that bus back and forth across town between Cliff's house and Roy's. But Tao and Gee were not financially prepared for me to take that international trip. In the meantime they paid me to assist Shi Tao in learning the English language. As we were growing closer and closer together, I taught her the basics.

Shi Tao eventually fell in love with me. I wasn't sure whether the feelings were mutual. Yet she did managed to convince me not to make the trip to Shanghi and we were together most of the time. We would go to the beach often late at night and walk along the shore, holding hands and talking. She would tell me all about communist China and her culture. I would in turn share with her the different aspects of the "American way" and how diverse our culture is. Although our relationship drew much opposition from Gee, because he wanted his daughter to marry within the Chinese race, Tao encouraged it. Not wanting to be the cause of any division within their close family unit eventually I backed off, out of their lives.

Meanwhile I was still waiting for that job at CSULA that had been promised to me. Lorraine, after seeing the adversity that I was experiencing, told me that she knew of an elderly woman who was looking for a student to come and live with her. She told me that the house was located in Altadena, in the eastern hills above Los Angeles. It was considered an affluent community. She said that the woman wanted two hundred and fifty dollars a month but that she was almost certain that an arrangement could be made. She told me that the elderly woman's name was Sally and that she was ninety-five years old. Since the experience with Mom Barnett was still fresh in my mind, I really was not too enthused about taking care of another woman in the latter stages of her life. But Lorraine suggested that I go see Sally, and since I knew that I was in no position to negotiate, I went because this presented an opportunity to get off of the indomitable streets. So, I reluctantly went to meet Sally and was pleasantly surprised to see this woman who looked like she was in her mid-sixties. She was alive, vibrant, beautiful, articulate and obviously cultured, having traveled the world.

Sally was a beautiful African-American matriarch who was sold on the Gospel of Jesus Christ. As we sat and talked the Spirit came upon me and I knew that this was where the Lord wanted me to be at that point in my life. Sally took an immediate liking to me and told me that I could stay there as long as I wanted. However she did tell me that her only granddaughter might bring her family to live there and if that was to happen that I would have to move. I respected her candor and honesty.

After moving in with Sally, my life began to change almost instantly. I would sometimes go to church around the corner and sometimes I would go to church with Sally who attended Crenshaw Christian Center. Over the years I had listened to the Reverend Fredrick K.C. Price on occasion and knew of the Faith Dome. But I had never gone there until Sally twisted my arm. There were often nights that I would borrow her neighbor's car in order to drive Sally to CCC, which is located in South Central. Her tenacity towards studying the Scripture sort of grew on me and for really the first time in my life I started to actually read the

Bible. I actually began to remember Scriptures. Sally taught me that it was through God that she could do the things that she was doing. It was because of God's grace that her life had been so long. She would tell me often that she knew that she was not going to be here on this earth much longer and that she wanted to turn as many people's lives over to the Lord's care as possible before her transition.

Lorraine, as in the case some years earlier when my lung had failed, was responsible for yet another important part of my development. Although I still continued to fall back into adverse situations, she always seemed to always know what I was experiencing and never gave up on me.

One day, while getting high with Roy we were watching television, a special news report interrupted normal programming. Apparently, Magic Johnson, the famous guard with the Los Angeles Lakers, was holding a major news conference to announce to the world that he had been infected with the HIV virus. Both Roy and I were literally in tears. He was our hero. We thought and talked about Rico, our mutual friend, who had recently died of AIDS. We remembered the pain that we shared with him, as we helplessly watched him deteriorate. There was not an inkling that suggested that Rico was gay. We asked ourselves how could this happen? Although we were both fairly intelligent and educated young men, we could not fathom a person that we loved and admired so much could fall the victim of this deadly disease. After Magic admitted that he had contracted the disease having unprotected sex, we immediately evaluated our own lifestyles, especially as it pertained to our sexual behavior.

Also during about that same time period we witnessed a news report about an incident that scared us somewhat, as I suspect it did most young African-American males. A black motorist was severely beaten by the Los Angeles Police Department. The Rodney King Beating was symbolic for one reason, in our lives, and that's because it was televised around the world. Countless African-American men have gotten the same exact treatment and nobody said anything about it, probably because nobody had a videotape recorder. My own life was in jeopardy on several occasions at the hands of those people who call themselves law enforcement officers. The prophet Malachi wrote, "So I have caused you to be despised and humiliated before all the people, because you have not followed my ways but have shown partiality in matters of the law" (Malachi 2:9).

We were not surprised that this was happening as we watched. But we were surprised at how the world and the media portrayed it as an aberration. We knew that this was not an aberration. In fact it's standard procedure for police officers in African-American communities to be abusive. We were taught by this observance the importance of racial sensitivity, as opposed to racial insensitivity. We had a renewed appreciation of the struggles and longsuffering that our forefathers had experienced to ensure that these atrocities would never happen to their children. Yet we were enlightened that although there was no longer a Civil Rights Movement, this movement was not complete.

Eventually after only about two months I had to leave Sally's home because her granddaughter and family moved into her house. I had anticipated this and was prepared to re-enter the world of the homeless. However Cliff asked me to stay at his apartment more often. I quickly learned that it is true that two can make it better than one. Cliff had quit his job at CSULA to pursue his dream of becoming a screenwriter. As I looked back at all those screenplays that he wrote, I can honestly attest that he possessed legitimate talent in that area. But I also knew that it would be extremely difficult for him to break into that profession. He knew that I was receiving food stamps most of the time so we made an agreement that I could sleep on his floor in exchange for buying the food. He and I had always gotten along well and this arrangement worked out fine.

Meanwhile I had been hired by the Recruitment Office at CSULA. It was a nice job and the one that I had been promised. But I was about to experience something that I had never experienced before—jealousy directed towards me from the other employees. I had been around the CSULA campus for a long time, and developed some rather fruitful relationships with people who could advance my career quickly. I had also become a role model student advisor for many of the young students on campus. There was another young African-American male who worked for the recruitment office who seemed uncomfortable and insecure by the fact that I had been hired. And most of his conversation was directed towards the director of the department and were attacks on my integrity and character. He and my immediate supervisor, an African-American female, conspired and launched a character assassination campaign against me. As I reflect on those times I can only assume the natural ambience derived from security in knowing who you are in Christ Jesus, sometimes is projected or perceived by others as arrogance. This, when a person is striving, trying to make it up the corporate ladder can be misinterpreted as a threat to someone else's insecurities and upward mobility. The resentment and negative energy that comes out from these adverse emotions is extremely destructive.

My job duties were to travel to the many Los Angeles

Community colleges and recruit as many students to transfer to CSULA as possible. Specifically I was told to concentrate on African-American males. I would make literally hundreds of presentations in a week's period.

At West Los Angeles Community College I met this student named Kathy. She was a very homely young lady about my age and I could just feel that she was filled with the Holy Spirit from the first moment that we met. I had known many spiritual women in the past, yet there was a significant difference about the way that Kathy witnessed. Later she would tell me that she was Apostolic. I was not familiar with this denomination, but I was quite impressed by her witnessing prowess. I agreed to go to church with her and she picked me up one Sunday morning at Roy's. Although very different than any service I had attended in the past, I must admit that those were some very holy people in that church.

The doctrine seemed to focus on the issues discussed by the Apostle Paul in his epistle to the Church in Corinth. There were many things that Kathy would and would not do because of her faith. I developed a small amount of discipline from my association with her. After she found out that I was homeless she invited me to occasionally sleep over at her apartment. Since it was Christmas time then she seemed to want me to be very much part of her family.

On campus Boo and I were becoming more and more involved with each other. However she was still involved with that young gentleman that she had been seeing for some years. But one day Boo and I could no longer deny our feelings for each other. We were both torn between two lovers. I was involved with Kathy, and Boo was involved with her boyfriend who was experimenting with Islam. Boo was struggling with her identity and seemed to find solace in our relationship. A time came when she and I had to let the other people in our lives go and we did for the sake of being with each other.

Finally I found a place in Cudahy, an Hispanic section of East Los Angeles. It was a small one-bedroom apartment which was all that I needed. Boo and I would spend a lot of time there and she was the first person who ever made me forget about most of those negative experiences in my past. We would make small talk about our future together, but she was not prepared to introduce me to her family because of my lifestyle. However I had met her father a few months before because he used to pick her up from school late at night, and appreciated the fact that I would stand with her until he arrived. Coincidentally her father and I had the same last name and had been born on the same day, different years of course. Boo was somewhat leery about my past drug use and the fact that I was a known womanizer. I tried to assure her that I had always used extreme caution in sex and had never used drugs intravenously. She still insisted that I take an HIV test and said that she would also. I refused her request, not because I thought that I might not pass one, but because Boo was still very much in contact with her then ex-boyfriend. Since she refused to break ties with him, I refused to take the HIV test, plus I felt that it was him and not her making that request. It was a pride thing. So out of pride I refused her wishes, and Boo and I broke up for the first time.

The Recruitment Office began to receive a lot of calls for me to come speak at various functions. This created an enormous amount of jealousy and animosity amongst my co-workers and eventually there was an all-out conspiracy to have me fired. After continued harassment from the very same people who hired me

I was forced to resign. Although I did not expect much loyalty from my supervisors and was somewhat relieved that I was out of there, I felt as if I had neglected those needy students in the South Central Los Angeles area. I remember seeing one student who I had established a judicious relationship with on campus, apparently he had decided to transfer there after attending one of my presentations. This gave me a sense of fulfillment.

But now I was once again without a job, and was very aware of what would come next. Also once again I began to wallow in my sorrows by drinking and smoking crack. One day while sitting at home getting drunk alone, the phone rang, it was this persistent gentleman who had been trying to get me involved in his muti-level marketing firm. He asked me to turn on my television, and that there was something that he thought I needed to see. So I did and the first thing I noticed was chaos—there were massive amounts of people on live television raiding stores and burning cars. All of a sudden Mayor Tom Bradley appeared, pleading for peace. Apparently the four Los Angeles police officers who had been charged in the Rodney King beating had just been acquitted by a Simi Valley jury. There was complete civil unrest and, although I was watching all of the initial stages of this violent release of frustration on television, I could smell and see the smoke from the burning building in South Central. I understood the frustration and I shared their pain. We all felt as though we were betrayed yet once again by the very system that promised us freedom and equality. But there was no freedom or equality demonstrated by these verdicts. So I understood that a demonstration, violent or non-violent, was in order. What I did not understand was why my brown and black brothers were burning their own communities to the ground.

Even though I really did not want to leave my apartment, I

knew that I would have to go back out to get some food. As I was walking to the chicken place I was stopped by the Cudahy police, demanding that I immediately return home. There was a curfew and I was in violation of it and they warned that if I did not immediately turn around and go home they would arrest me. After asking me where I lived they took my address and followed me home.

Several days passed and I had literally been under house arrest. Each time I tried to exit my apartment I was approached, it seemed, by those same two cops, demanding that I return home. In a lot of ways that solitude and separation from the world afforded me an opportunity to realize my inward spiritual condition. I had been getting sort of homesick again, a feeling that I had experienced every so often. So I decided that when my tenure expired in that Cudahy apartment, I was going to hop another Greyhound bus and begin another cross-country journey.

So a few days after the riots were over, I sold most of my possessions and stored the rest of them in Cliff's apartment and left Los Angeles en route to Richmond. This was a journey that I had been on so many times before, always looking for something that I knew wasn't there...but still searching and very much not knowing what to expect. Yet still I knew that I did not want to be alone in Los Angeles during that initial recuperative period. I was fed up with all the injustices. I was tired of all the childish games Boo was playing. I was tired of the continuous helicopters and sirens, always paranoid—thinking they were coming for me. Psalm 119:28 warns us, "My soul is weary with sorrow; strengthen me according to your word." My soul was disturbed, and quite honestly I was tired and needed rest.

CHAPTER THIRTEEN

DEPARTURE

After arriving in Richmond for the first time in about three years I noticed that much had changed. My mother picked me up from the bus station and I could not help but notice that she had aged. The beauty of her youth began to give dominion to Mother Nature. This was a wake-up call in some ways, because I finally began to realize just how long I had been gone. The first issue that she and I discussed was my plans. I informed her that I was not really sure what my plans were but I wanted to try to make it in Richmond for awhile. I assured her that I had no plans to remain there for any extended period. Basically I was seeking refuge from the chaos and isolation that the vastness of

Los Angeles represents. Very candidly she told me that Richmond was not the place to be trying to make it and I knew what she was implying.

My oldest sister Sandra seemed happy to see me and was openly pleased to witness my Bachelor's degree diploma. She had recently gotten a divorce from Comer and appeared to be getting her life back in order. At first my mother's longtime companion Herb seemed uneasy and made me feel as if I was invading his territory. Understandably so because my mother had been living alone for a long time and I assume he had become the man of the house per se. Since he really did not know me or my intentions he probably was feeling sort of threatened. But I expeditiously assured him at my mother's request that I was not going to be staying long. After hearing me say this he seemed to relax around me somewhat. Herb's daughter Teresa and I had gone through school together when we were kids. She and I were always good friends in those days and she would always pull me to the side and tell me that I really was not the "type" to be getting in a lot of trouble. I knew that if Herb was anything like his daughter Teresa he had to be a righteous man. He was intelligent and a God-fearing man which in my opinion carried a lot of weight, eventually we came to respect each other in a profound way. Later it turned out that he was quite easy to talk with. Junie and his wife Loretta had just had a baby girl, and I was about to meet her for the first time. Alyna Jade was a beautiful child but she did not favor anyone on our side of the family, nonetheless she was a doll.

Cynthia was skeptical about my sudden return, however I immediately sensed that our relationship had changed for the best. I discerned that both of us were more mature and educated.

She became my friend and confidant. We had never been that close in our entire lives. Our relationship had always been strained, even more so in recent years because I did not make it to her wedding. I had never previously met Kevin, her new husband, and she was about to give birth to a baby herself. Cynthia, by then, had been living in Washington, D.C. for some time and had told mom that when I came home she would come down and spend the weekend with us.

My second week at home I started to work a long-term temporary job. My entire family was extremely surprised that I started to work that fast, especially since they really did not know what to expect from me. Although I had always held a job over the years, they were unaware of this fact. Their memories of me had been from earlier years when working was the last thing on my mind. They only knew how I used to be, and I had never had the opportunity to change their opinions, but I knew that their opinions would ultimately determine how long I would be in Richmond.

It was unfortunate that I had to prove myself to my family. Yet I knew that it was necessary if I wanted to stay there. John 6:6 tells us concerning Jesus' intentions to feed the five thousand, "He asked this only to test him, for he already had in mind what he was going to do." Even though I felt as if I was under the microscope, it didn't bother me because I knew what I was going to do. I was determined to show them that I had grown up, I had become a man. Yet still I walked a fine line around them.

One day while downtown, I ran into an old school acquaintance named Michele. Throughout junior and high school she was considered by some to be the most beautiful girl around. But then, in my opinion Arnie was. Yet Michele ran a close second. We had always been friends and we had not seen each other since high school, but the years had been good to both of us, at least to our outward appearances. We began to date and become very close in a rather short period of time. We did not spend as much time together as we would have liked because of our schedules, and neither of us had cars which made it all the more difficult. But we talked a lot on the telephone and quickly found out that we had many things in common. Michele had been through a lot of adversity, in terms of homelessness, drug and alcohol addictions. We could relate to each other because our journeys through life had been similar. I could sympathize with her lifestyle, and visa versa.

One night while Michele and I were watching a movie at my mother's house, it became very late, neither of us knew how she was going to get to the west side where she lived. So I invited her to stay over. The next morning while my mother was getting dressed to go to church she came up to my room where she kept her hats in the closet. After she entered the room and saw Michele and me in the bed together, she had this disapproving look on her face. She ordered us to get dressed and to come downstairs where she would be waiting. From the look on her face you would have thought that I had killed someone. Concerning the instruction of children the Scripture warns us, "Only be careful, and watch yourselves closely so that you do not forget the things your eyes have seen or let them slip from your heart as long as you live. Teach them to your children after them" (Deuteronomy 4:9). My mother came from the "old school" and she firmly reminded us of that. I felt badly for both my mother and Michele because I knew that I had initiated all of this and accepted full responsibility for what had transpired. I had been living away from home for so long, and it is true that no matter how long you may be gone away from home, you will always be a child to your parents. Nonetheless that experience brought Michele and me even closer.

Throughout the entire period that I was home I continued to think about California. For several reasons—one was the fact that I had been accepted into the University of West Los Angeles School of Law, and I had no intentions of passing on that opportunity; and secondly I was unsure of what, if any, relationship I still had with Boo. Yet I knew that deep inside I loved her and I owed it to myself to bring some sort of closure to it. She was calling me almost every day and she was coming very close to graduating. I could sense from our conversations that she was slowly maturing. I wanted to believe that she loved me as much as I loved her. When I left California I think that she realized that I was serious about not only our relationship but my future as well. Boo knew that the longer I stayed in Richmond, the more likely it was that I would not be returning to Los Angeles. She was right, as I had begun to seriously consider staying in Richmond with Michele who had been trying to convince me that we had a future together.

Although I did not disagree with her about our future together, I knew that I did not want to stay in Richmond but she was adamant about staying there. Her mother had custody of her daughter, so she didn't want to leave. In California, where Boo was in the final stages of completing her degree in Heath Science, I felt a sense of belonging and a yearning to complete what I had started.

The inner man convinced me that I was in love with both Michele and Boo. I was now torn between not only two lovers but two cities as well. But for some reason, deep inside of me, I did not feel a sense of loyalty to either of them. I felt this way about Michele because over the years she had become somewhat street-wise and independent, yet she was equipped with alluring personality. But I wanted to get away from the street- wise types. And I didn't feel a sense of loyalty to Boo because she was not as mature as other women who had been in my life, and I knew that as long as she continued to be involved with her ex-boyfriend in any way I was not going to feel secure in any relationship that we shared. I had left an intimate relationship with Kathy to be with her, and I did not want to go through that experience again. So I knew that if I returned to Los Angeles it would be to attend law school.

Michele and I had been together by then for a couple of months, one day I could not find a knife that I had had for a lot of years, and had a sentimental attachment to. I figured that Michele had stolen it because she had been the only other person who spent time in my room. This was the defining moment in our relationship. This was the excuse that I was looking for to end my relationship with Michele.

I accused her of stealing that knife and abruptly ended a relationship with another decent young woman that I really never gave a chance to develop in the first place. I remember her crying and pleading with me not to end it. She adamantly proclaimed her innocence to my deaf ears. She even offered to take the responsibility for stealing the knife if I would reconsider our union, but to no avail. I finally realized during those last phone conversations that I represented stability and security in her life then. Michele knew that if she stayed with me for a little while longer that I would take care of her for the rest of her life.

A couple of days after I ended our relationship, I came home from work and found the knife on the kitchen counter. My mother told me that my niece had found it upstairs in the drawer in the bathroom. Apparently I had placed it there one day while I was drunk. There was this extreme irksome feeling inside of my soul after that because I had accused Michele of taking that knife because of her financial problems. And all the while I had hidden the knife from myself. It hurt because Michele was willing to take the blame for something she knew that she did not do, for the sake of saving our relationship. Even though Michele had been through a lot of negativity and was street-wise, I felt at that moment that I did not deserve her. 1 John 1:9 says, "If we confess our sins, he is just and will forgive us our sins and purify us from all unrighteousness." I asked God first for His forgiveness, and then I asked her and she gave it. All of my life I had been accused of things that I had not done, and there I had accused her of something she had not done. And I knew that I had destroyed forever that strong bond that we had formed.

My childhood friend Malcolm and I did not spend much time together during my stay in Richmond because he was an extremely busy person. Apparently he had taken over his father's disc Jockey business. Carroll could no longer function in that capacity as he once could, and Malcolm was forced to take the lead in operating Epps Disco. But Malcolm and I did get to spend some time together before I left Richmond, just as if nothing had changed in all of those years. Unfortunately he was in the final stages of his marriage with Donna.

Comer, now my sister's ex-husband, was estranged from the rest of the family. Apparently he had done a lot of evil to my family because they would get extremely agitated whenever he came around. But after he heard that I was in town from my nephew "CL" he stopped by to pick me up one night. Herb and I were sitting in the kitchen when my mother came in with a pernicious expression on her face and told me that there was someone outside who wanted to see me. I went to the door and noticed that it was Comer. He said that he did not want to come in but asked if I would like to take a ride with him to get a beer. Since I had not seen him in years, and in the past we had been somewhat close, I agreed. Yet on my way out the door my mother insisted that I leave my house keys with her. Since I knew what she was thinking I did not put up much resistance.

Comer showed me the room that he was renting in the Churchill section of Richmond. This was an area that I was very familiar with because my entire family had delivered newspapers there when I was a kid. When I returned home and entered the front door, my mother was standing there with this look of relief.

Thanksgiving was rapidly approaching and it would represent the first holiday that I had spent with my family in a lot of years. Several of my aunts from New Jersey were coming down to spend that day with Big Ma, in the country. She was, by then, my lone surviving grandparent and was ninety-two years old. That massive farm was now relegated to a house in the woods. Big Ma still knew who everybody was, and she and my father's last living brother John, still lived out there in the midst of nowhere. Yet, this little house in the woods and its surroundings represented serenity in its purest form. The entire time that I was there I could hear those voices of my childhood, and visualize my cousins and myself playing in those now vacant grassy fields. There had always been this extreme closeness between my father and his siblings. It was an enviable closeness that had somehow eluded me and my siblings. It was evident that when my aunts looked at us they saw him. During the times that we spent with my father's family there were unexplainable emotions that would encompass all of us. "Rise in the presence of the aged, show respect for the elderly and revere your God. I am the Lord" (Leviticus 19:32). As I was leaving that day I remember my mother gesturing towards me as if to make sure that I said good-bye to Big Ma. And as I said my good-byes to her I couldn't help but wonder if that would be the last time that I would see her alive.

The closer it got to Christmas, the colder it was getting, and the more I was thinking about Los Angeles. It was my intention to start law school in the spring so I really was in a hurry to get back to LA. I gave my mother some money and asked her to purchase a one-way bus ticket there. Since I was not constrained by dates, I believe that those long cross-country bus rides afforded me the necessary time I needed to meditate. But also those long journeys provided me with time to contemplate my next course of action. So Mom did as I asked and I planned to leave just before Christmas. Unlike my previous visits there, this time my siblings tried to talk me out of leaving, even though I was aware that my Divine destiny was pulling me in another direction. But there was something significant about my stay in Richmond this time. I do honestly believe that my family developed a genuine appreciation for me. They may have formed somewhat of an attachment, this was something that I was not used to. They all knew that it was highly probable that they were not going to see me for a few years.

Once again before I left, each of my siblings made a conscious effort to ask me to reconsider; however I believe my mother was torn. On the one hand I think she wanted me to stay, yet on the other hand I knew that she wanted her privacy and house back. Nonetheless I had made up my mind that I was leaving and I did, but this time I had money in my pocket.

After arriving in Los Angeles I went to Cliff's apartment to store my belongings. Since I did not have another place to stay I offered him some money, which I knew he needed, and he agreed to allow me to sleep on his floor until I could arrange for a more permanent living situation.

Ralph, one of my mentors at CSULA, had introduced me to an administrator with the State Employment office in Los Angeles. She in turn referred me to a Vietnamese case manager named Nancy who was an employment counselor. To my amazement Nancy took a liking to me and said that she could get me into this program called Civil Unrest. This was a government-subsidized program that was created to help minorities who had lost their jobs or experienced some deprivation resulting from the recent riots. The program entailed that either the State, County or City governments provide job training to the disadvantaged minority participants by allowing them to work at their job sites. Since I had participated in the CETA program some years earlier, I was somewhat familiar with these sorts of programs. I immediately started working in the Consumer Affairs office located in the Hall of Administration in downtown Los Angeles. This job afforded me the opportunity to get my foot in the door, so to speak, with the County of Los Angeles.

There I could undoubtedly meet people who could help me. Also I could acquire the necessary job skills that would prepare me for the future that I was much in search of, not to mention that it was a full time assignment that would pay me the money that I needed to support myself.

My job duties required that I prepare and analyze financial statements and prepare financial documents for managerial budgetary decisions. The county of Los Angeles was experiencing extreme fiscal hardship during that time, and my immediate supervisor Derrick was in charge of preparing the budget for the Consumer Affairs office. He taught me many things about the preparation of financial spreadsheets. He was also a part-time law student, which intrigued me, and we seemed to have a lot of other things in common.

I had been informed by the financial aid department at the University of West Los Angeles Law School that I had to sit out for another semester or two because of some outstanding loans that I had incurred as an undergraduate at CSULA. So the entire time that I was participating in the Civil Unrest program, I was trying to save the necessary money to go back to school. I was all too aware that if I stayed out of classes for an extended period, the likelihood of my returning was slim to none.

I had rented a couple of rooms in the mid-city area right off of Crenshaw Blvd. It was pretty close to Boo's parents' home. She was graduating soon and I was very conscious from my own experience that she needed to be alone to concentrate on her studies. My place was situated in the back part of this Christian woman's house, and she was extremely nice. But as soon as the rainy season arrived, my entire place was flooded after only two months. My landlord was accommodating, after a little pressure from the people that I worked with, she eventually gave me back my deposit plus some extra money to move. I quickly found another place not too far from there in the affluent Lafayette Square Park District. For African-Americans, this neighborhood was the Beverly Hills section. The house that I moved into was owned by an elderly well to do woman named Ella. She said that she had bought the house from Dorothy Dandridge, the premiere Black Diva of the 1950s. Ella was a ritzy and shrewd businessperson who also took a liking to me immediately. She rented me the prized back greenhouse/converted room which in my opinion was the best room in the house. It was the only bedroom on the bottom floor and was situated directly adjacent to the swimming pool and Jacuzzi. I had my own bathroom and walk-in closet, plenty of solitude. Her house was in a direct route to my employment too.

Since my employment in the Civil Unrest program was rapidly expiring, I had intensified my job search. While doing so I had managed to meet some extremely influential people in county and city government. A county supervisor introduced me to a professional headhunter by the name of Madeline. She in turn introduced me to a high-ranking finance administrator, with the city of Los Angeles, named Paul. Both quickly became mentors and involved me with numerous community causes. They enlightened me on something that had eluded me most of my life, which was that I had a social responsibility to donate some of my time to community functions. It was during that time that a virtuous woman with a divine gift of compassion crossed my path, her name was Lurma. Jesus' mother Mary said, "My soul glorifies the Lord and my spirit rejoices in God my Savior" (Luke 1:46). She taught me how to love in a spiritual way and I knew that I was blessed that God had put her in my path.

At the EDD office Nancy told me about a test that was coming up regarding a position within the State's EDD office as a State Disability Examiner. This was a well- paying permanent job with lots of benefits, something I was not used to. The State was anticipating hiring a lot of people for that position so I took the examination. Nancy said I had just as good a chance at securing one of those positions as anybody else. After scoring high on the test, I was placed in the highest percentile and was assured that I would eventually be hired. But there would also be an extended waiting period.

Meanwhile I had developed a cordial working relationship with a woman by the name of Sarah. She was the contact person for the Civil Unrest payroll and was located in the Department of Community and Senior Services county office. In more than one of our many conversations Sarah had mentioned that her department hired student workers on a regular basis. She went on to suggest that she would give me a reference to come and work there after my employment expired with Civil Unrest. She instructed me to come in and speak with her supervisor Johnny.

Her suggestion took an enormous amount of pressure off of me. Even though Ella was basically a good person by nature, she was also a businessperson. She did not allow us to be late with our rent and I personally witnessed her evict several tenants. Since I had been evicted more than once, I wanted desperately to avoid that process as long as possible.

I started working for the County Department of Community and Senior Services as a financial assistant to Johnny, who was the County's Grant Administrator. I was once again responsible for compiling data and preparing financial spreadsheets. Derrick had trained me well and I had become a very seasoned administrative assistant. The entire floor that I worked on was filled with professional accountants. They all had been working together for many years before I got there and appeared to be a very tight knit group. They made me feel extremely comfortable in their environment. My schedule was Mondays thru Thursdays 6:00 A.M. to 4:00 P.M. I enjoyed every Friday off. In fact the entire department operated that way. My responsibilities included transporting millions of dollars in checks between the Hall of Administration and the Department of Community and Senior Services. That was the most satisfying job that I had ever held in my entire life. I knew that it did not come any better than that. Never before had I ever worked for an employer who was as interested in teaching me than Johnny. Although he was an extremely important individual, he always seemed to make time each day to spend with all of us who worked for him. Johnny always reminded me not to relinquish my ultimate goal of becoming an attorney.

At home one morning I received a phone call from my mother, informing me that my ex-brother-in-law Comer had been shot to death. She told me that they had found his bullet-riddled, bludgeoned body partially decomposed in an abandoned house used for shelter by crack heads. Apparently there were several other people killed that same weekend. Our childhood friend Michael's wife was also killed. Comer was an extremely hyperactive individual who had a hardhead, but he also had a good heart and a drug and alcohol problem that he would not address. So death and destruction were imminent. 2 Kings 8:10, says, "Elisha answered, "Go and say to him, "You will certainly recover; but the Lord revealed to me that he will in fact die." Comer's demise shocked no one, not even his own immediate family. His addiction had grown out of control early in his life. Yet he and I had always seemed to remain good friends, and we shared a special relationship. In some ways I knew him better than most of the family. And in my opinion he was an individual who needed help. However he refused to admit it. In my life I have met literally hundreds of people just like Comer who will not allow themselves to receive help. But inside they are screaming for help, and nobody hears. Maybe they refuse to hear. I have learned that most gifted and virtuous people are so involved with their own lives that they sometimes forget, or choose not to hear those who are less fortunate and those who might bring them discomfort or embarrassment.

Some years before Comer was murdered, I had watched my roommate Clint's troubled life lead him to committing suicide. Nobody, including myself, knew that things had gotten that bad. In Comer's case however I believe some people, including myself, were aware that his early death was inevitable. And in my opinion, this was a terribly wasted life.

Roy once again began to hang around more and more. And because of my conscious thoughts of what had happened to Comer and Clint, I began to view our friendship in a different light. He too was now experiencing an awful, vile drug pestilence. I found myself somewhat obligated this time to help him. He was homeless so I let him sleep on the floor most nights. He had a car and was traveling back and forth from San Gabriel Valley where he thought that he had a girlfriend. Most of the time that he came over he had drugs with him, which meant that I got high for free; although I was weaning off of that stuff, I was not making a conscious effort to keep it away from me. Roy eventually went to jail for traffic warrants, and when he got released his circumstances overwhelmed him and he was forced to return to East St. Louis where he had roots. This was a decision that I encouraged because I did not want my good friend to end up like Clint. But also it was a sound decision because he had become a burden to me and Cliff. So Roy, the last of my heavy drug using partners, with whom my relationship had legitimately grown from genuine dislike to Agape love, departed from Los Angeles. When I watched the Greyhound bus pulling out of that station I knew deep in my soul that was probably going to be the last time I saw him. However, just as I had experienced with the departures of Johnny B, Champ, Big James and some others, I knew that I would recover and just kept striving with my college buddies Ray and Cliff, putting those chapters in my storied life behind me.

CHAPTER FOURTEEN

SITUATION SUPER BOWL

During 1994 Ella was evicting tenants at a high rate. But there was also a core three or four of us that had remained constant. There was Millie who was the matriarch of the residents, Craig, from Madison, a stockbroker and an alcoholic, and there was John, from Australia who worked all the time and was rarely at home. In fact I was the only resident that was there most of the time so Ella delegated to me, in exchange for minimal rent, the manager duties. For the writer of proverbs tells us, "Blessed is the man who listens to me, watching daily at my doors waiting at my doorway" (Proverbs 8:34). Ella trusted me and knew that she could depend on me to look after her place.

VOICES OF MY FATHER

In January 1994, the state interviewed me for that position at the State Disability Insurance Department in Culver City. They then shortly thereafter informed me of a starting date. Yet I had mixed emotions because of the attachments that I had developed with my co-workers at the county. I had established a certain amount of job security that I was reluctant to relinquish. Johnny was not only my employer, mentor, and friend, but he had become a confidant as well. In many aspects I viewed him as the motivator that I needed so desperately in my life then. And I believe he looked at me as his surrogate son, always stressing to never give up on my dream of becoming an attorney. He told me not to make career decisions based on money, or the potential to make money. But there were others whose opinion was also important to me. I had developed a special spiritual relationship with Christina, an elderly Filipino widow who I worked very closely with. She told me often that I would be successful one day, and threw a party for me when I left. That was also a first for me.

I had a one-week grace period between jobs. Throughout my first day working for the state, I had this feeling that something just wasn't quite right. The position itself was extremely different from anything that I had done in the past. On the first day when I walked through the door I felt as if I was at an auction, being paraded around like a piece of meat. I quickly noticed that there were only two other African-American men working there and one of them was openly gay. Even though there were over one hundred people working in that office, the ethnic and gender make-up of that place comprised eighty African-American women, a couple of white males, and the rest Hispanic and white females. I had worked around a lot of women in the past, and had been rather comfortable in doing so, but for some odd reason I knew that this group would be somewhat different, probably based on the looks that I was receiving.

Six of us had been hired at the same time. We had to attend a training program to learn what it was that we would be doing for the state. Since in the back of my mind I knew that my ultimate goal remained to become an attorney, I did not allow myself to get caught up in office politics. Yet a peculiar occurrence happened while I was having lunch one day at the Training Center with another trainee named Crystal. Obviously streetwise, she made some rather straightforward sexual advances toward me. Although I was somewhat flattered I did tell her that she was not my type. She inquired what I meant by that statement. So I went on to tell her that in the past I had dated women from various cultures and races. She became very belligerent and accused me of being a "Wayward Brother." She accused me of betraying my race, and said she felt that since I was a young, intelligent, upwardly mobile brother who was about to attend law school, that I owed it to the sisters to share my resplendency. Yet I was perplexed about her contention because I had never explained to her my feelings about that one-way or the other. I reacted to her aggression in a nonchalant manner, thinking that my comment to her had served its purpose—which was to squash her unwanted advances. However her agitated posture towards me spilled over into the classroom when she made some derogatory statements in front of the entire class about my personality and character. During one of the breaks I asked the instructor if he could speak with her and curb her aggressive behavior towards me, and he did.

Upon our return to the office on Monday, Crystal, her supervisor, my supervisor, and the manager, coincidentally all black women, went inside of the managers' office for a long time. No one knew what the nature of their meeting was but I had this feeling that they were talking about me. Apparently, Crystal had told them that I had attacked her verbally. She told them that I had made some negative comments about her background. She inferred that I had said that women of her race were not good enough for me. This was another character assassination—something I had experienced before. But this time it was really personal. I assured them that I loved my African Queens and reminded them that my mother is one. I then went on to explain that I had rejected Crystal's unwanted sexual advances. I felt that they believed the part about the unwanted sexual advances yet they began to ask me personal questions that had nothing at all to do with my job training or the incident with Crystal. They bluntly inquired about my preferences in women, how I felt about their education and race. They asked me how I spent my free time and who I spent it with. I explained to them that all of my life I had been indifferent towards the race of any woman that I was involved with. I told them that I never really considered race a factor when courting a significant other. But these women were African-American women who seemed to be becoming hostile towards me, something I was not used to. They apparently felt that I was another young, arrogant, successful black male who no longer felt he needed or wanted a sister to share his life with. In all actuality I really just wanted a job. My life was already extremely complicated enough without this, and they wanted to turn this simple occurrence into the office soap opera. The only reason I said what I said to Crystal was to try to dissuade her from pursuing a relationship with me. My career with the State

Disability Insurance Office went downhill at an accelerated pace after that. "Those whose teeth are swords and whose jaws are set with knives to devour the poor from the earth, the needy from among mankind" (Proverbs 30:14).

Meanwhile in the summer of 1994 Ella had allowed this notably crazy individual to move into our home. He immediately started literally terrorizing not only the people living there but also the neighbors. We started having neighborhood meetings about him and the best plan of action to get him out of there. The police knew about him but said that there was nothing they could do. He made numerous threats on my life, which rattled me somewhat, because over the years I had learned not to underestimate anyone. He was six feet seven inches tall and weighed well over three hundred pounds. Reflecting back I now know that I should not have been scared of him because Moses wrote in Deuteronomy 1:17, "Do not show partiality in judgment; hear both small and great alike. Do not be afraid of any man, for judgment belongs to God. Bring me any case too hard for you, and I will hear it."

Eventually Millie moved out. John was contemplating moving also. Craig was looking for another place but I really did not have another place to go. I did not want to move because of the volatile situation that I was experiencing at work. I found myself spending a lot of time with my "play sisters," Helaine and Carma. However, they were finding me unbearable because I began to stress and drink a lot. The harassment and gender discrimination I was experiencing at work had become intolerable too, and I was forced to take a stress leave of absence. Grace, my supervisor, had wrongfully filed a negative formal evaluation on my job performance after only several hours on the job, so I knew that my time around there was short. I could have gone back to the county but my pride did not allow me to do that. I did not want Johnny and the rest of them to know that I had failed.

During my distress on the job I sought the counsel of an EEO Advisor that worked out of the Santa Ana branch office of EDD. The advisor's name was Mildred, but she preferred to be called Marti. At first our relationship was strictly business, however it became rather quickly more than just cordial. She seemed to use the professional information that I shared with her for personal gain. I should have taken heed to her doing this because Luke wrote, "Do not be misled: 'Bad company corrupts good character. Come back to your senses as you ought, and stop sinning; for there are some who are ignorant of God, I say this to your shame'" (Luke 15:33).

At home my room had been broken into, and Ella and everybody else knew who had done it. Several of my expensive suits were stolen, along with some jewelry. Ella just kept telling us the same thing that she had been telling us for several months which was she was working on getting the crazy man out. But I knew, from my own experience with unlawful detainers, that it would be a lengthy process. There was another problem that came along with all of this—the agitator needed someone to blame for his troubles, and he chose me. Then his aggressive behavior escalated into acts of violence and he threatened to kill me on several occasions. Add this to all the troubles I was having at the job, my life had become extremely chaotic.

Since I was unsure what this insane person was capable of doing, the intelligent action for me to take was to make myself scarce around there, at least until Ella could get him out. Although she had agreed to allow me refuge at her mansion in the Pomona Hills during this uncertain turmoil, it was too far for me to travel to and from work.

In my vulnerability and out of fear of losing the rest of my suits, I moved most of them to Marti's condo in Santa Ana. She knew that this arrangement was just temporary, but she also knew that my job situation was extremely volatile and was probably coming to a rapid end. It was inevitable because of the amount of harassment I was experiencing, plus the fact that I had filed counter paperwork alleging the harassment with EEOC. Marti was extremely knowledgeable about the state's employment and termination policies and used them in our relationship in an assertive manner.

One day in October my mother called and told me that she and Herb had decided to marry. This brought joy to my heart even though most children never really want to see their parent remarry—especially if they knew their other biological parent. However in this instance we all knew Herb and considered him to be a fine gentleman. He and my mother had been together for many years and both of them were getting up there in age—they deserved each other at this point in their lives. Herb is an extraordinary God-fearing man and my mother could have done a lot worse. Since she had retired a year earlier and since her groom-to-be was equally yoked, it was time for them to enjoy the finer things that the rest of their lives had to offer.

So I informed my supervisor that I needed a few days off to fly to Richmond for my mother's wedding. Marti insisted that she pay for my airline ticket and I went to Richmond for a few days. When I arrived, most things were just as I had left them a couple of years earlier, but I did have the opportunity to meet my new nephew K.J. for the first time, and he was a big active toddler for his age. His father Kevin does stand about 6'5," and his mother Cynthia is about 5'11." Even though K.J. was barely more than a year, he looked like he was about three or four years old.

The night before my mother's wedding, my brother Junie and Kevin took me to this nightclub and we were all drinking and as usual I consumed too much. When Junie and Kevin wanted to leave early I insisted on being left there. This was another grave mistake because the next thing I knew I was in the county jail, calling around to see if I could get someone to come down there and pick me up. But while I was waiting the next morning for my brother, I noticed that one of the jailors looked familiar. Later I came to find out that she was the sister of my late ex-brother-in-law Comer. I knew that there had to be a reason why our paths had crossed this way and this gave me the opportunity to speak with her about how my good friend had gotten himself killed. After speaking with her, I was able to bring some closure to the incredible emptiness left inside of me by the death of my good friend. "No man has power over the wind to contain it; so no one has power over the day of his death. As no one is discharged in time of war, so wickedness will not release those who practice it" (Ecclesiastes 8:8). My brother finally picked me up, I attended the beautiful wedding, and left Richmond.

Marti picked me up from the airport in Los Angeles. Even though we had started to spend a lot of time together, there was definitely something about her that was making me more and more uncomfortable by the day. All of my life I have been emotionally attracted to Spiritually-led women. Marti acted very much on impulse. She was physically bigger than I was and because of her past profession as a prison guard, at times she could actually be intimidating. She seemed to be experimenting with her sexuality. Unfortunately I was not interested in her that way. Yet her entire affiliation with me had become solely an expression of her sexual fantasies. She would continually remind me that because she was in her mid-forties her biological clock was ticking. Regardless of my feelings, she often said that she wanted a child by me and wanted to have sex as much as possible. I often reiterated my desire and need of a spiritual friend but she appeared to be indifferent to what I wanted and needed. Because of my living, working and financial situations, I had become extremely vulnerable. She knew this and used her dominance in our relationship in a violently assertive manner.

Since Marti was basically financing our relationship, she felt that she was entitled to certain perks, which usually included sex. She had become overly possessive of me and would exert violent tendencies, especially when I could not give her what she wanted. She was oblivious to the fact I was experiencing severe hardship and stress. She was just waiting for the state to release me from my commitment with them so she could tighten the reins. She knew that I was being constantly harassed by my employers and co-workers. She knew that I was experiencing a very volatile and adverse condition at home and that I did not want to sleep there. There were nights when I could not give her what she wanted because of stress. Yet she was insensitive and would strike me in the face as if I was a little kid. She knew that I did not have a car and did not want to catch the bus late at night from Orange County. She knew that I did not want to go home, she knew that if I went there late at night that my life was in danger and she would threaten to take me there anyway.

And as we were en route, if I fell asleep on the freeway she would put both of our lives in danger by striking me in the face. She knew that I was afraid of the police yet she would often drive to the Santa Ana police station and threaten to go in there and tell the police that I was hitting her.

We were both alcoholics and she would buy me all the whiskey, cocaine, and marijuana that I wanted, thinking that it would stimulate my sex drive. When it did not she became agitated which manifested into violence. Marti had a penis fetish, often mentioning Lorena Bobbitt. She threatened to cut my penis off on numerous occasions while I was asleep because she said it was useless. But because I knew her propensity towards violence, I refused to take those threats as empty ones.

Sure enough, as expected, the day in early January 1995 came when I was released from my commitment with the state. Oddly, this came only days after they were notified by the Federal Equal Employment Opportunity Commission that I had filed a formal complaint charging them with gender discrimination and sexual harassment. Every party involved knew that this was a retaliatory measure against me because of the conversation I had had with Crystal, and the fact that I had filed a formal complaint against them. However there was not much I could do because I had only been on the job for less than a year.

Marti, with her opportunistic attitude, quickly began to make arrangements for me to move in with her. Even though I knew that I did not want to be forced to move in with her, I also knew that this was an option I had to keep open. Deep inside Marti had homosexual proclivities. In fact she had admitted to being involved with another woman in the past. All of her close friends were homosexuals. Since she had been a prison guard in the past she told me that she was very used to violence. She told me that she and her friends wanted me to participate in orgies, and said that once I was sleeping naked in her bed she had some friends over looking at me.

After that I began to scrutinize her every move and was discreetly looking for a way out of that debilitating relationship. But when I stopped coming to her house on the weekends she started to stalk my house, late at night.

On Super Bowl Sunday, 1995, I was at Marti's condo hoping to just have a relaxing day watching the game. However she had other intentions for us that day. She wanted to go to a Super Bowl party over at one of her friends' houses. Suddenly there was that Voice in my head again, this time telling me not to go to the party. Listening to that Voice I adamantly told Marti that I did not want to go. She insisted that I go and once again threatened to put me out on the freeway if I did not attend the party with her, so I reluctantly went.

When we arrived at the party there were four other people there—a female couple and a male couple. Even though I had never in the past discriminated against anyone because of their sexual preference, I was angered after one of the male homosexuals propositioned me. This is what I was trying to avoid by not wanting to go to the party in the first place. We all were drinking heavily and I said some things, insisting that I wanted to leave. Marti seemed to be more mad at me for rejecting the gay males' advances than she was at him for making them. They all were looking at me as if to say that they wanted me to participate in something they had previously planned. I told Marti that I would be waiting for her in the car because I had begun to feel uncomfortable. A few minutes later Marti came out angry, agitated and drove us back to her condo. The writer of Psalms wrote, "Everyone has turned away, they have together become corrupt; there is no one who becomes good, not even one" (Psalms 53:3).

When we arrived back at her condo she was very mad and agitated, and when she had gotten that way in the past she became violent. When she went into the restroom I laid on the floor and went to sleep. When I awoke she had cut my pants off and had a pair of scissors in one hand and my penis in her other hand. Marti, who weighed at least fifty pounds more than me was straddled over my waist. I immediately started hitting her in the face until she fell off of me. After she fell, I got up, put on some shorts and grabbed my remaining personals and ran out of there. On my way to the bus stop, for some stupid reason, I threw those cut pants in the trash. And with nothing on but athletic shorts, I caught the bus back to Los Angeles.

A couple of days later I received a message on my voice mail from an Orange County Detective requesting that I call her regarding Marti and the events that transpired at her condo on Super Bowl Sunday. So I saved the message and went to speak with an attorney friend of mine by the name of Hank Sands. After listening to the message he called the detective and asked her what it was she wanted to speak with me about. She said they wanted to talk with me about what had happened at Marti's condo. The detective went on to inform Hank that there were no charges pending at that time but agreed to call him in the event that there would be charges filed in the future. Hank assured her that if they did file any charges he and I would come to Santa Ana and surrender myself, thereby allowing me the opportunity to fight these charges from the streets.

Shortly after that I started to receive many bizarre telephone calls and messages. But I had an idea that those phone calls were coming from Marti. I began to pray that this odious, possessive, sexually obsessed and despicably evil woman would just leave me alone. Shortly thereafter I felt a sense of relief because I never heard from her or the detective again and finally I could start to put my life back together.

That unfortunate situation with Marti enlightened me about the dark world that is no doubt controlled by the evil forces that I knew existed but refused to acknowledge. It also showed me that there are so many lonely people in this world who are experiencing pitifully isolated depression, because those people seem to possess a distorted belief that the world owes them prosperity in every form. Since Marti had been the dominant figure in our relationship, she felt as if she owned me. This escapade also taught me that I could no longer indulge in just casual relationships. There was never an intent on my part to spend a long period of time with Marti. Although she knew that she represented financial security for me, in her mind she was trying to buy love and companionship. She was somehow hoping to convince me into remaining in that turbulent and melancholy relationship.

Ella finally got the "Crazy Man" to move out. I had started working for a telemarketing firm in Hollywood and was feeling good about the direction that my life had started to move. I was attending both West Angeles Church of God in Christ and Crenshaw Christian Center regularly. God had blessed me with discernment and I was beginning to understand certain truths about His Word, and myself. The Lord had become my best friend and I was withdrawing from those people who were not conducive with my reverberated spiritual experience. The writer of Psalm 18:28 wrote it best, "You, O Lord, keep my lamp burning; my God turns my darkness into light."

One day in April I was impelled to go and visit Boo. I was interested in how her spiritual voyage was faring and I could not call her because she had changed her number. She had said that she was going to do that the last time we spoke, because I was too much into the world. As immature as I thought she was, I knew that she was right. When she opened the door I could feel her spirit, and she was quite pleased to see me. Something happened that had never happened before—she invited me in the house. I had met Boo's stepfather at CSULA, he coincidentally had the same last name as me. And we were born on the same day, different years of course. He was notably gifted with wisdom. After all those years of knowing Boo I was finally getting the opportunity to meet her family. I met her beautiful mother and sisters. I met her intelligent brother. Her mother possesses this dazzling beauty and appeal that is augmented by her obvious love for Jesus Christ. In fact she immediately started to witness to me—handing me some faith literature. They were all very nice people and reminded me of those days I had spent with Rhonda and her family.

Boo and I had been friends for a very long time. The way that our relationship evolved over the years afforded each of us the privilege of knowing things about the other that no one else knew. She knew of the many vices that had controlled my life for so long and wanted to help me overcome them. Although she had left me twice in the past, both times to resume a relationship with her ex-boyfriend, I could not seem to muster up enough resentment towards her—especially since our relationship had grown from being acquaintances to having a legitimate Agape love for one another. She had become my sister, and shared my heirship, for Paul wrote, "Now if we are children, then we are heirs—heirs of God and co-heirs with Christ, if indeed we share in his suffering in order that we may also share in his glory" (Romans 8:17).

One day while she and I had been praying and talking, we realized that our future together had become auspicious. We made certain vows and spiritual promises to each other. But for me, a spiritual commitment was born in my heart and I asked Boo for her hand in marriage. Very much to my surprise she accepted. We both prayed for God's anointing to be placed on the covenant and we prayed that he provide for us the direction, and lead us towards His purpose for our lives together. Boo wanted to wait for awhile before she told her parents about our engagement, and since I knew her reasons for the delay I did not pressure her, especially since she was the best one to make that kind of decision. We even agreed to hold off on having sex, as we should have, because we did not want to interfere with the blessings of the Lord.

There was still this pestering vice that was lingering in my life. That Voice that had been there with me for most of my life kept telling me that I needed to get rid of that vice. Yet this time that Voice also told me that if indeed I wanted the blessing that I deserved, and if, in fact, I wanted my life to be significantly different, I would have to conqueror and destroy that vice now— before I married Boo.

There had been many conversations about my drinking problems between myself and my sisters Carma and Helaine. So after Carma made some phone calls and pulled some strings, we decided that the best course of action for me to take then would be to check myself into this drug and alcohol rehabilitation center called Acton, located in the Antelope Valley. But for a successful program I would have to live there for ninety days, and for the first couple of weeks I could not have any contact with the outside world. All I could think about then was Sunstreet and how that dope-infested place was. The mere thought of spending my summer with a bunch of alcoholics and drug addicts was not my idea of fun.

Once I told Boo about my intention, she was ecstatic since we both knew this would be best in the long run for our relationship. We also knew that if I did not take care of this now that I probably never would. However it was not Boo who convinced me that I was doing the right thing, it was Helaine. She was the one who assured me that when I got out of that place she would be there to help me get back on my feet. I had always valued her advice because she and her sister Carma, were the most reliable people I knew. Even my trusted male friends Cliff and Ray could not give me those feelings of security.

The day was rapidly approaching that I was to enter Acton, but not fast enough because I allowed the evil one to convince me that I was making a mistake. Subconsciously I began to think that I was entering a jail type of situation—something I vehemently did not want to do. I knew the type of people that were going to be there, and quite frankly I did not want to be around them. So at the last moment I decided against going to Acton. Carma and Helaine were disappointed with me after that. Boo was too, but I believe she felt that I had everything under control. But she did not know that I was very much out of control, out of spiritual balance.

A few days later, I had been drinking heavily and decided

to attend this after party. While walking home I passed this neighborhood crack head who knew me. He asked for a loan, undoubtedly because I was wearing an Armani suit. Of course I did not give him any money. After thirty seconds later I heard someone shouting, "Put your hands up on top of your head and turn around slowly." This was a familiar command to every young African-American male. So I did, and noticed two LAPD officers aiming their revolvers at my head. After frisking me they asked for identification, something I never took with me whenever I went out late at night. After telling them my name they ran a warrant check on me and discovered that I had a $50,000 arrest warrant issued by Orange County. The warrant was for assault with a deadly weapon, with an intent to commit great bodily injury. After that they treated me as if I was the most dangerous criminal on the face of this earth.

I tried to explain to them that all of this was some sort of mistake. Yet I was aware that I was dealing with the most infamous, atrocious, and contemptuous policemen in the world; common sense and prior experience told me to just shut up if I wanted to keep my life. All I could think of then was Boo. I knew my destination was the county jail, and once there anything was likely to happen. But I felt that Orange County would not come and get me, but then Los Angeles County extradited me. Suddenly I knew that I was in trouble, mostly because the first bit of street knowledge I had acquired from the brothers when I first moved to California was never go to jail in Orange County. Their voices were so surrealistic inside my head. But they also had warned me that a black man does not have any chance of true justice inside a courtroom in that county, and once again in my life I found myself afraid, very afraid.

CHAPTER FIFTEEN

DESTINY

After only a few minutes inside the Orange County Jail, I sensed this would be a repugnant experience. As in most jails the officers immediately separated us by race. As infamous as Los Angeles County Jail is, they were not as segregated as OCJ. Yet I was still housed in a desegregated part of the jail. There were several other blacks housed with me in this ward. Even though I knew that the charges levied against me were serious, I felt that I would only be in custody long enough to be arraigned. After that process I thought that I would be released on my own recognizance. However at the video arraignment, I quickly found out that these people were not playing fair. I mentioned to the public defender representing me that there had been a verbal agreement between Hank Sands and the Santa Ana police detective that if they were going to press charges against me they would let us know. It was brought to the court's attention that indeed the investigators' report showed that there had been an agreement, but the court seemed indifferent about that agreement, and I was told to go back to the holding cell until the public defender contacted Hank Sands. The public defender never came back and I was told by the deputy that another court date had been set in two weeks for a preliminary hearing.

Upon arriving back in my cell I phoned Hank's office myself, only to speak with his secretary, who informed me that he wanted $2,500 to come down and speak with me. Considering my financial situation then, that was very bad news and it was virtually impossible to come up with that amount of money. I was aware that I needed a real attorney because if I relied on the public defender I was headed straight to the penitentiary. That Voice inside of my head kept instructing me to call my friend and neighbor Bill McKinney, who I knew specialized in criminal law, to come and represent me, but my pride did not allow me to do that. I did not want him to know that I had gotten myself into a situation such as this.

There were many public defenders who came by to speak with me during the various stages of my trial. Even though they all said that they believed that I was not guilty of the crimes that I was charged with, they also warned me that if I went to trial and lost I would only be subject to one year in county jail. Nonetheless they also told me there were several factors against me that needed special consideration. One pivotal factor, deserving much thought, which should be considered colossal was the fact that I was a black man on trial in Orange County. In fact I was told by more than one public defender quite candidly that they had never seen a black man win a trial in that county. Jesus Christ taught us himself about racial prejudices in John 4:9, "The Samaritan woman said to him, 'You are a Jew and I am a Samaritan woman. How can you ask me for a drink?'" For Jews did not associate with Samaritans." Another obstacle they told me I would have to face in the courtroom was the fervor over the O.J. Simpson trial which was in its contemptible stages during this same period of time. Apparently the public defender's office felt that the district attorney's office would portray this as a classic domestic violence abuse case, even though they were aware that I was most likely provoked into my actions.

Those analogies made me second guess what I already knew I had to do. All of my life, in some sort of manner, I had conducted myself in a way as to resist racial and judicial injustice. And now I was facing a trial in which even those who were representing me knew that I did not have a chance at winning, based not only on my race, but the politically conservative climate and the fervor brought on by the O.J. Simpson trial. I remember thinking to myself what a terrible time it must have been for literally millions of black men going through the judicial system during that time, as if it was not already bad enough for black men trying to gain justice in this country. They even acknowledged that it was unrealistic, given my background, that I had acted unprovoked. In their words "I did not fit the profile."

A public defender named Mr. Swanson was delegated the task of representing me on trial. He was a very notable, young, intelligent attorney who had a winning track record. Yet he was very candid and informed me of what it was I was up against. He even went as far as to warn me not to expect a fair trial. He said the political fervor in that county would supersede the due process of law. He said that there would be resentment towards me for several reasons—one being that I was black, another being I was in Law School. He felt that this trend for resplendency would not work in my favor. Nonetheless, he did admit that I was probably not guilty and never once tried to pressure me into taking a deal. I respected his candor and decided that if I had any chance at winning this trial, he would have to be the public defender in the forefront.

We went into trial somewhat reluctant, but I still felt that at the end the truth would prevail. There was no one in the courtroom to support me morally. And Helaine was the only person who seemed to even care about what was happening with me. She had brought down one of my best suits to the courtroom a couple of days before my trial started. She was the one who had gone over to the house on Victoria to get my things. She had stored them in her father's garage. She was even willing to come and testify as a character witness; however Mr. Swanson did not subpoena her, for some odd reason.

Mr. Swanson warned me beforehand about my speech and demeanor during trial, so I remained conscious of that the entire time I was in the courtroom. During the jury selection phase of the trial, I quickly found out what it was that those public defenders had been telling me. There were no African-Americans at all in the jury pool. And Mr. Swanson made reference to this fact in his opening statement, but the court's transcript did not reflect this. Ms. Shade, the deputy district attorney, immediately set out to portray me as a vicious criminal. This was her job, of course, and was expected. However just to sit there and listen to all those lies was extremely difficult for me to endure. Psalm 101:7 says, "No one who practices deceit will dwell in my house; no one who speaks falsely will stand in my presence."

During the jury selection, a lot of questions were asked concerning domestic violence. Also, as expected, there were many different viewpoints. Since I did not know how to pick a jury, and since I felt a sense of confidence from my attorney, I allowed him complete autonomy during this process. There were jurors who admitted during questioning that they could not in good conscience give me a fair trial. There were also jurors that said that I was probably guilty even though no evidence had been presented. A question was raised in regards to the O.J. Simpson trial and whether any of the perspective jurors had already come to a conclusion as to whether he was guilty or innocent. The entire jury pool raised their hands and we knew at that moment that we had virtually no chance at winning.

But I went ahead and allowed my attorney to select a sitting jury. It was comprised of all Anglos, except for one Hispanic. As I looked in their faces I could not help but feel that this was all a masquerade, they had already made up their minds as to my guilt. I felt as if I had murdered a prominent member of their uppity Orange County community. A community that I knew nothing about and in fact did not even know my way around. I could count on both hands the amount of times that I had been in that community. And yet in the eyes of the law I was being tried by my peers. Those people did not resemble any peers I had ever known or had in my life. This was a moment in that I must admit I felt extremely helpless. It was ludicrous for me to think that those people would see me as the person that I was, and not as the vicious black criminal that the district attorney was portraying me as. Yet I had subconsciously fooled myself into thinking that I would somehow still get a fair trial, all the while knowing deep inside that I would not.

During the break, right before opening arguments, Mr. Swanson came in to tell me that the court had precluded both sides from talking about our past. In normal circumstances a ruling such as this would benefit most defendants, but not in my case, because although I had been arrested before, the only convictions in my past were for drunk driving. There was a tremendous amount of achievements, unlike that of the stereotypical normal young black male, in my past and we knew that if I had any chance of winning this trial my accolades would have to be highlighted. But the judge in my opinion established early that there was indeed going to be a conviction in this trial.

Marti, no doubt a dominatrix, was the first person to testify in the case. She got on the witness stand and told a calculated, concocted and rehearsed version of what had transpired that night, which by then was seven months ago. There was absolutely no truth whatsoever to anything that she said happened once we returned to her condo. In fact her testimony sounded as if it had been written by a Hollywood screenwriter.

The police officer that had answered the call that night was the next witness to testify, but he was not that detrimental to my defense. In actuality he helped me a little because he contradicted some of Marti's testimony. A significant part of his testimony was not heard by the jury because the judge cleared the courtroom. The officer testified that, based on what he was told by Marti, a misdemeanor battery had taken place. He also went as far as to inquire why had a felony assault been alleged. Of course no prudent explanation was given.

The prosecutor then called Marti's personal physician to the stand to speak about the injuries that she had sustained. From what Marti had told me about this doctor in the past, her testimony should not have been deemed credible. Also she would have said anything that zealous prosecutor wanted her to say. Her testimony hurt my chances a lot, and with the exception of Marti's testimony, was the most fabricated.

The defense phase of the trial started next and since Mr. Swanson chose not to call any character witness, the entire defense was riding on whether the jury believed me or not. I quickly learned a viable lesson—I told them the entire truth. Any reasonable person could conclude that it was improbable that I acted without provocation. Marti was twice my size, and the jury and everybody else in the courtroom could see that. Nonetheless I tried with every fiber in my body to convince the jury that I had acted in self-defense. Something inside of me was saying that they believed me. I told the jury how I had gone to sleep on the floor. I told the jury how this sadomasochistic woman had cut my pants completely off. I told the jury that when I awakened I felt a sharp cold object on my penis. I reminded the jury about Lorena Bobbitt and what she had done to her husband, and how Marti threatened to do the same to me one day. I told the jury how I had grabbed Marti by the back of her neck, and hit her continuously until she fell off of me. I told the jury how I collected the remainder of my things and left her apartment. I told the jury how in the past this woman had forced me to have sex with her. I told the truth, the whole truth, and nothing but the truth so help me God.

The court would not allow my attorney to present a lot of evidence that would go towards my credibility. He had declared that it was imperative that he be allowed to introduce testimony that I was enrolled in law school, in an effort to show that I was a credible witness. It was compulsory that the jury hear the resplendency that had occurred in my life. He even acknowledged that it was highly probable this jury knew nothing about African-American males, except how the media portrayed us. Unfortunately for me the district attorney, a zealous woman, had successfully gotten the Judge, also an imperious woman, to rule in her favor most of the time.

Although the trial went in favor of the prosecution in terms of the rulings, I still felt that my public defender did a reasonably good job in the courtroom. The jury also appeared to have some misgiving about the prosecutions' theory because they deliberated a full day before returning a guilty verdict on both counts. They convicted me of an assault with means likely to produce bodily harm, with a specific intent enhancement of great bodily injury. As I sat inside that holding cell, waiting to be transferred back to the county jail, I could not help but hear that same Voice inside my head. It was that same Voice that was always giving me advice, directing my path through life. Yet there was never any real discernment on my part. Matthew warned us concerning this, "But if your eyes are bad, your whole body will be full of darkness. If then the light within you is darkness, how great is that darkness!" (Matthew 6:23).

Knowing that I was on my way to state prison, I had some loose ends that needed to be secured in my personal life. Since there was a grace period of about forty days between the time I was convicted and the sentencing date, I began to open up with those people I thought were the closest to me. The Lord says, "These are the things you are to do: Speak the truth to each other, and render true and sound judgment in your courts; I do hate this" (Zechariah 8:16-17). I had told the truth to the jury, and now I had to come clean with the people who loved me the most.

When Boo heard about what had happened to me she cried, yet some of her comments led me to believe that she was more concerned about herself. But when I spoke with my sisters Carma and Helaine, they were more concerned about whether I had received a fair trial. Because they knew, and everybody else who really knew me—knew, that I was not capable of committing a crime that would commit me to prison. Suddenly I knew that I really did not even know Marti. She really did not know me either. Yet we had been intimate—if you can call a brief sexual experience that. The bottom line was I realize that God knew who I was all the while. I had gotten to that point by my disobedience to the Voice of God. And naturally my spiritual relationship with God instantly became my impetus. My family was somewhat supportive, even though they were actually unable to help me. My mother especially was helpful, in that she told me that whatever time I would be doing she would be doing with me. Never in my life will I ever forget those words because this gave me some inner strength, and I knew that if I was going to rise above this situation I would have to turn my attention to God.

Later I called my good friends Bill McKinney and Morris at their law firm. They wanted to know why I had not called them in the first place. Since I knew that it was pride I gave them some odd reason, yet they referred me to an appellate attorney in San Francisco by the name of Cliff Gardner. I contacted him and he told me that once I was sentenced to request that he be appointed to represent me on appeal, which I did.

At my sentencing hearing Ralph Dawson came to speak on my behalf. However, as the judge indicated, my public defender should have called character witnesses during the trial, and whatever Ralph might attest it was probably too little too late. Nonetheless, Ralph told the court that he had known me for more than ten years and had never known me to be a violent person. He said that it was highly probable that I had acted in self-defense and that I was telling the truth during trial. The court thanked Ralph for his testimony and politely excused him, as if to say he could leave the courtroom. But Ralph stayed and witnessed exactly what the court did next. The court went on to sentence me to three years for the assault, and four years for the great bodily injury, both to be served consecutively for a total of seven years in the California State Penitentiary, forthwith. There were white men in the cell who were being sentenced to thirty days in the county jail for committing crimes ten times worse than the crime for which I was wrongfully convicted.

As I sit in prison now, still waiting on the United States Court of Appeals for the Ninth Circuit to rule on my appeal, I cannot avoid but ponder how my life had come to this. Yet I knew that God had a purpose for me, as He always had. On April 16, 1996, as I laid in my bunk about two-thirty in the morning, God spoke to me in a Vision, much as He spoke to the prophet Ezekiel. The Vision called me to preach the Gospel of Jesus Christ. And now I have no choice in the matter. I count my present sufferings as joy and thank my father that He has chosen to set me apart in order to impart Divine Wisdom and Truth. I must be about my Father's Business.

I don't receive many letters anymore. Boo and the rest of my so-called friends are all part of a distant memory. More importantly, my quest to serve the Lord has become auspicious. And as God has promised He has also broken down the walls and barriers, and He has destroyed all the yokes. In the meantime I am going to keep on praising the Lord and I know that it is going to be alright as I continue to press forward toward the goal, always keeping my eyes on the prize that He has called me Heavenward.

"Brothers, I do not consider myself yet to have taken hold of it. But one thing I do: Forgetting what is behind and straining toward what is ahead, I press toward the goal to win the prize for which God has called me heavenward in Christ Jesus" (Philippians 3:13-14).

CHAPTER SIXTEEN

NO CHOICE IN THE MATTER

Now, on the other side of prison because both the Ninth Circuit Court of Appeals and The United States Supreme Court ruled "harmless error" in determining the merits of my appeal. However it is difficult to understand how a mistake made by the trial court that sent an innocent man to prison for six years can be deemed "harmless." "There is surely a future hope for you, and your hope will not be cut. Listen, my son, and be wise, and keep your heart on the right path" (Proverbs 23:18-19). After graduating from Seminary, I realize that I never wanted to be an attorney in the first place. Sunshine had warned me concerning "The Box" some years ago. Now I understand completely where living in that box can lead you. All of my life I had been living my life trying to be part of the "American Dream." For the first time I knew that that dream was not afforded to me. Since there were obviously no apparent secular reasons for my predicament; I knew that it had to be a Divine objective. I thanked God for setting me apart that I might be prepared for special service.

While I was away, besides writing this book, I founded and incorporated a faith-based nonprofit organization with the intent to inspire people to persevere through adversity. Pond my release I was quickly voted in by the board to serve as its president and CEO. We provide mentors and positive role models to anyone who needs them. As I have attested throughout my life, God has always provided me with an angel to guide my way. Even my homelessness can be attributed to free will. My distorted intellect manifested into false pride—and that false pride was leading me straight to destruction and death.

It wasn't until I stepped out of the instruction of my youth that I became wayward. So many of our youth today do not have positive role models and accordingly go astray. Fathers are leaving the home—some intentionally, but far too often against their will. Mothers can be mothers to young boys and girls but mothers can't be fathers. This is the main fabric behind our youth joining gangs. Human nature dictate that we need a sense of belonging, we need to be accepted by our peers. We need to be loved by our family and friends. And far too often our youth satisfy these needs by positioning themselves in the local gang. Yet, others satisfy these needs through alcohol and drug use. The latter was my case. Good thing I grew up fast and modeled myself after Frank I. Carter, Sr. Family unity and positive role models is important in the lives of our youth. That is what we promote at The Conversion Project. "But if you do warn the righteous man not to sin and he does not sin, he will surely live because he took warning, and you will have saved yourself" (Ezekiel 3:21).

No one should have to go through unnecessary negative experiences in order to find their way through life. I had to write this book because I made too many mistakes—even though at times I knew The Way. My parents had taught me right from wrong. I had to write this book for all the men and women around the world who cannot see The Light, nor do they know The Truth. I had to write this book for those people in hospitals, in gangs, in the boardroom and those hooked on drugs. I was compelled to write this book for people in unhealthy relationships—relationships with abusive bonds that will lead you to destructive behavior, prison or death. I had to write this book for those in prison—justly, or unjustly. I needed to write this book for my soul. I had to write this book for the fatherless boy or girl. I had to write this book to inspire the single parent. I had to write this book because I had no choice in the matter. God told me to write this book. "From everyone who has been given much, much will be demanded; and from the one who has been entrusted with much, much more will be asked" (Luke 12:48). If you read this book you will have a moral obligation and spiritual responsibility to go out and tell somebody.

As you have probably discerned from my journey, I have always been blessed, even though at times there were many stumbling blocks making it difficult for me to stay on my feet. People who know my story often want to discuss problems about their wayward child, brother, sister, or significant other. After listening to their individual stories it seems that I always hear my own. When counseling, I advise them to always keep their eyes on the prize. That's what I did and I did not turn out that bad. Yet, that's not all that I say to them because often times during my journey I kept my eyes on the prize and still managed to go astray. Psalms 16:7 tells us "I will praise the Lord, who counsels me; even at night my heart instructs me. I have set the Lord always before me. Because he is at my right hand, I will not be shaken." According to this Scripture it is the Lord who counsels me. I attested to the fact that during my significant years I have always valued sound advice. And since true wisdom only comes from God it is in Him that I seek it. "But the wisdom that comes from heaven is first of all pure; then peace-loving, considerate, submissive, full of mercy and good fruit, impartial and sincere" (James 3:17). I promise to touch on the subject of wisdom in more depth in my upcoming book.

My relationship with my family is better than it has ever been. Actually, if it had not been for my mother's love and compassion during my incarceration I am sure it would have been more difficult to make it through. My family is very important to me, as your family should be to you. Oftentimes during my journey I had forsaken my family. Frankly, I had given up on ever receiving the kind of love that I thought was due to me. And subconsciously because of my estrangement I had blamed them for most—if not all of my trials and tribulation. One cannot make another person love them the way that they want to be loved. You can only allow another person to love you according to their ability to love. It wasn't until I accepted that fact and had come to myself, much like parable of the prodigal son, that I began to realize that it was never the fault of my family for anything that was going awry in my life. The Apostle Paul wrote in his first letter to Timothy "If anyone does not provide for his relatives, and especially for his immediate family, he has denied the faith and is worse than a believer" (1 Timothy 5:8). My family had always supported me no matter what I wanted to do. They did not agree with most of my decisions when I was a rebellious teenager, but they always picked me up when I fell down.

When I was away, it was my mother who answered each and every one of my phone calls. Even though she couldn't begin to fathom what I was experiencing—she seemed to know when, what, and why I needed to talk. Now our relationship exemplifies respect, mutual admiration and unconditional love. She has forgiven me for my rebelliousness, she has become my friend and confidant, as well as my loving mother. Moses wrote, "Cursed is the man who dishonors his father or his mother." Then all the people shall say, "Amen!" (Deuteronomy 27:16). My siblings are my closest friends. They all have impeccable wisdom and I was blessed just by being their little brother. Sandra has demonstrated time and time again what a true spiritual woman should be like. Junie, although not his brother's keeper, would not have a problem assuming that role. My conversations with Cynthia are invaluable. In most ways she understands me better that any other member of my family.

As I reflect on the many lessons that my parents taught me and my siblings, the one that has paved the way for me is to, not only be loyal to your family, but also love them unconditionally. Solomon wrote, "The proverbs of Solomon: A wise son brings joy to his father, but a foolish son grief to his mother" (Proverb 10:1).

It amazes most people who know me, how I've managed to live

this long and prosper—given my vicarious drug use during this journey. By man's terms I should have died a long time ago. Once again I can only attest that it was by the grace of God that I am not dead. Luke 21:34 says "Be careful, or your hearts will be weighed down with dissipation, drunkenness and the anxieties of life, and that day will close on you unexpectedly like a trap." In case you do not know we serve a sovereign God. He affords mercy and grace on whom He wishes. It's not that I am special by any means, but, He chose to bless me with that level of grace and mercy and He'll do the same for you? In actuality He will bless you with His grace and mercy according to your measure of faith, but you have to ask for it. I haven't had a drink of alcohol, nor have I consumed any drugs in almost ten years. But I am sure that most of my vexation was a direct correlation to my indulging in mind altering substances. Psalms 84:10 says "Better is one day Your courts than a thousand elsewhere; I would rather be a doorkeeper in the house of my God than dwell in the tents of the wicked."

One morning over nine years ago, I woke up and decided I did not want alcohol or drugs anymore and never touched any of it since. My thinking changed and what had fascinated me about that lifestyle—no longer did. "Do not conform any longer to the pattern of this world, but be transformed by the renewing of your mind. Then you will be able to test and approve what God's will is—his good, pleasing and perfect will" (Romans 12:2). Now comes the bondservant!

BOOK AVAILABLE THROUGH
Milligan Books, Inc.
Voices of my Father $14.95

Order Form
Milligan Books, Inc.
1425 W. Manchester Ave., Suite C, Los Angeles, CA 90047
(323) 750-3592

Name_____ Date _____

Address_____

City_____ State____ Zip Code _____

Day Telephone _____

Evening Telephone_____

Book Title_____

Number of books ordered___ Total ....$ _____

Sales Taxes (CA Add 8.25%) ....$ _____

Shipping & Handling $4.90 for one book ..$ _____

Add $1.00 for each additional book...........$ _____

Total Amount Due......................................$ _____

☐ Check ☐ Money Order ☐ Other Cards _____

☐ Visa ☐ MasterCard Expiration Date _____

Credit Card No. _____

Driver License No. _____

Make check payable to Milligan Books, Inc.

_____   _____
Signature   Date